The Bilingual Revolution Series

TWO CENTURIES OF FRENCH EDUCATION IN NEW YORK

The Role of Schools in Cultural Diplomacy

Jane Flatau Ross

The Bilingual Revolution Series

TBR Books
New York

TBR Books is a program of the Center for the Advancement of Languages, Education, and Communities. We publish researchers and practitioners who seek to engage diverse communities on topics related to education, languages, cultural history, and social initiatives.

CALEC - TBR Books
750 Lexington Avenue, 9th floor
New York, NY 10022
www.calec.org | contact@calec.org

Front Cover Illustration: Jonas Cuénin

Cover Design: Nathalie Charles

ISBN 978-1-947626-47-8 (hardback)

ISBN 978-1-947626-16-4 (paperback)

ISBN 978-1-947626-17-1 (eBook)

Library of Congress Control Number: 2019952057

Dedication

To my husband, Alfred Ross, and children, Adrian and Caroline, whose boundless enthusiasm and encouragement gave me the extra strength to complete this project, and to my parents, sister, and brother who have always inspired me.

Praises

Jane Ross has not only written a marvelous history of the Lycée Français de New York, bringing to that analysis deep insight gleaned from three decades teaching in the school. She has also illuminated what this story reveals about French cultural diplomacy, French-American relations, and the challenges educators have faced adapting French ideas about education to new times and diverse locales across the globe. This book makes an important contribution to the study of international education, dual language learning, and a fascinating dimension of New York City's history over the past two centuries.

—Herrick Chapman
Professor of History and French Studies
New York University

Jane Ross tells the story of Two Hundred Years of French Schools in New York as a compelling and unique chapter in the history of bilingual education. In Ross's account the New York schools are similar to other bilingual ventures in the goal of truly advancing student's bilingual capacity and understanding of both cultures, but also unique in the significant role of the French government's tight control of these U.S. based schools making them truly an outpost of the education offered in France itself. It is a compelling story for anyone concerned with bilingual and bicultural education.

—James W. Fraser
Professor of History and Education
New York University

Education has played a major role in shaping French identity. What happens when it becomes international? Jane Ross' intimate knowledge of French education in New York allows her to draw on that case study to tell a fascinating story about the evolving role of education as a key instrument of French soft power. Her book should become required reading for anybody interested in French soft power.

—Jean-Marie Guéhenno,
French Diplomat, former Under-Secretary-General
at the United Nations

The French government maintains over 490 Francophone schools around the world, of which one of the most renowned is the Lycée Français de New York. Jane Ross taught there for thirty years. Her engrossing history of French education in New York is thus a unique blend of insider experience and scholarly investigation.

—Robert O. Paxton,
Professor Emeritus of History,
Columbia University

In this wonderfully engaging book Jane Ross restores to view a little-known dimension of French educational rayonnement in the US. A must read for anyone seeking to understand the cultural ambitions of global France today.

—Alice L. Conklin,
Professor of History
Ohio State University

With deft scholarship and engaging prose, Ross clearly lays out 200 years of French education in New York City, enriching our understanding of French history, Franco-American relations, and the rich potential of global schooling initiatives - including increasingly necessary heritage language programs - in creating truly intercultural citizens.

—Kimberly Potowski
Professor of Hispanic Linguistics
University of Illinois at Chicago

In this elegant mix of memoir and serious historical and scholarly investigation, Jane Ross directs our attention to the achievement of French schools abroad in accomplishing important and evolving cultural work for the French nation since the 19th century. Her analysis is rich and complex, for in such schools as the Lycée Français de New York, the educational experience is not uni-directional or even merely bi-lingual: American students learn French; alongside them French students learn English, and speakers of languages other than French and English learn both. Ross has a firm hand both on the historical role of French education abroad over two centuries— that of preserving various cultural and political articulations of "Frenchness"

-- and the layered, complex, global education inevitably taking place in the classrooms of French schools overseas today. For anyone who has studied between two languages, who has been a student of France, French heritage, and culture, and who is deeply interested in the transformative power of international education, Two Centuries of French Schools in New York: The Role of Schools in Cultural Diplomacy is a must read.

— Celeste Schenck
President
The American University of Paris

FOREWORD

From French Identity to Global Education

What a fine idea Jane Flatau Ross had at the beginning of this beautiful study, to evoke the image of her French ancestor Henri Chapiers, who at age fourteen joined the troops led by the Marquis de Lafayette. The young Frenchman set off bravely to come to the aid of the American revolutionaries—claiming to be a surgeon! Behind him, more obscurely, we can discern his mother, a midwife who knew how to read and write. Chapiers subsequently decided to remain in the young republic. Thus began a familial tradition that has nourished the author's imagination and inspired both her vocation as a teacher and her determination to explore the teaching of French in New York over the course of two centuries, in order to understand its importance and its meaning.

A Palpable Connection

From the outset, one aspect of Ross's work that makes it so immediately engaging is the palpable connection linking the researcher closely to her object of her study, a connection that is reinforced throughout the book and constitutes its guiding principle. We meet Ross first as a young American student in Grenoble, where she discovers French education at the Lycée Stendhal; next, we see her working as a substitute teacher at the Lycée Français de New York, the prelude to a thirty-year-long career at the school, where she would hold several different positions. In particular, Ross contributed directly to the introduction in 1998 at the Lycée of the *Option Internationale du Baccalauréat* (OIB), a program that in the United States allows high school students to simultaneously fulfill the graduation requirements of the French "Bac" and the American Advanced Placement Program. Ross left the Lycée in 2003 to devote herself to a new adventure, the French Heritage Language Program, undertaken by the FACE Foundation (French-American Cultural Exchange), even though it initially seemed of scant importance. Her discrete presence and her nonetheless focused and effective efforts at the heart of this association were in keeping with a familial heritage that, while feeding the questions that fuel her research, also contributes to lending her account here its vividly concrete character.

Yet Ross's personal involvement in the story she tells never prevents her from maintaining a necessary scholarly distance, not least by virtue of the range of the sources she consults, from all the expected archival collections to interviews with a variety of figures, both American and French. Indeed, Ross's systematic reliance upon her interviews reveals anew just how interesting oral history can be. Ross's approach accordingly enables her to articulate the relationship between her case study and overarching issues, as her subtitle, *The Role of Schools in Cultural Diplomacy*, expresses perfectly. Ross's persistent effort to balance fieldwork with the institutional perspective is likewise among her work's other great strengths.

The Paradox of the French School System

Ross begins by recalling the distinctiveness of French education outside France vis à vis the analogous approaches of other developed countries. The French system is unusual in not being reserved only for expatriates, to enable their children to pursue the national curriculum. Rather, the French approach is one of the most important means for protecting and developing French linguistic culture—indeed, it is a weapon of diplomatic "soft power." For this reason, education in French outside France itself is largely open to local students as well as to foreign students attracted to French culture. Overall, overseas educational institutions in which French nationals constitute the majority of students are very rare.

Yet while highlighting this reality, Ross also shakes up received ideas—and this is by no means the least interesting aspect of her work. The most familiar image of French education is its steep hierarchy with, at the summit, the leading role played by the national Ministry of Education and, in line with this hierarchical structure, an emphasis on uniformity and simplicity that is at once the system's strength and its weakness. Yet throughout her book, Ross reveals the diversity and the complexity of the French educational system abroad—for example, the fact that a great many of its institutions abroad, if not the majority, are private, with a board of directors independent of the French authorities.

The system of French education abroad was initially developed under the aegis of the Mission Laïque Française (the French Secular Mission, founded in 1902), which was likewise independent of the French government, even if de facto informal links between them have always existed. More surprising still, the Mission was founded in the context of colonial Madagascar, where French military authority maintained a powerful presence, with the objective of developing a secular ("republican") school system to counter the denominational education undertaken by a variety of missionary communities. The Mission Laïque later succeeded in remodeling itself in the Middle East in order to compete with Catholic schools—another vector of French influence—before arriving in the United States and in other countries around the world with the highly developed ability to adapt to local contexts that remains one of its priorities. By contrast, the Agence de l'Enseignement Français à l'Étranger (AEFE: the Agency for French Education Abroad) is administered in France directly by the Ministry of Foreign Affairs, comprising three kinds of institutions, each with a very different status: AEFE schools may be directly managed (*en gestion directe*), contracted (*conventionné*), or accredited (*homologué*). Such variety contradicts the image of a uniform system.

Ross's exposition of such nuances reaches an inevitable apex of paradox when she considers the terrain central to her research: New York City, with its flourishing array of French-language schools, none of which is administered by the French authorities. The oldest of these, the École Économique (Economical School), is not merely deeply rooted in the city but one of the originating institutions of the New York public school system—its founder, Baron Hyde de Neuville, was a royalist in the days when Napoleon ruled as Emperor of France. Meanwhile, one of Ross's principal observations is that while there have been, over the years, numerous sources of tension between the New York's Lycée Français and French governmental officials, nonetheless they have not prevented the school from becoming in the eyes of many, as she writes, a "citadel of French culture in New York City." The most powerful testimony in support of this aspect of the Lycée's reputation is provided by Maristella Lorch, an Italian-born American (and hence the mother of Italian-American children) and founder of the Italian Academy for Advanced Studies in America at Columbia University. As Lorch tells

Ross, "My daughters looked out the window and they said, 'The Loire this morning is in bad shape,' but it happened to be the Hudson. They didn't even know that we lived in New York!"

This surely shows the degree to which the Lycée as an independent establishment in New York plays a major role as a source of French cultural influence in this key city. Yet the situation is not quite that simple, and Ross's work in fact goes far beyond examining the role of French education abroad in French diplomacy—the book's subtitle is reductive, it does not express all that she shows. Maristella's daughter did not become French, despite her passion for the Loire and her identification with France. Fully American and just as fully open to the world, as an adult she has come to hold an important job—in New York City. The mixing of the three groups of students at the school—native French speakers, Anglophone Americans, speakers of other foreign languages—leads de facto to cultural cross-fertilization, despite the strong imprint of French schooling. Some of Ross's interview subjects attest to this truly double culture, at once both French and American, while some go even further, speaking of a genuine "global education."

What was implicit in the twentieth century has become explicit in the twenty-first: in other words, Ross shows how the resolve to provide a French-American education—and, beyond that, a broader global education—all the while safeguarding French identity, leads at the same time to changes in how the Lycée is organized and to the adoption of a program instigated by the French authorities, the OIB.

What the Future Holds

One final remark. At the end of her concluding chapter, Ross cites a report from the French Cour des Comptes (the Court of Audit, which fulfills a role similar to that of the American Comptroller General) stating that French education abroad today stands at a crossroads. The French government, she writes, "must be willing to make bold choices and major adaptations in order to 'breathe new life' into the network of French schools around the world." Some of the responses to this challenge may be found precisely in Ross's previous chapter, such as the French Heritage Language Program noted above, which is already being implemented in several New York school districts and is already well supported by the French embassy. First, schools in this program reach new constituencies that traditional networks have never touched and will never be able to reach. Of still deeper importance is that the program's classes develop a pedagogy that strives for optimal coordination of the French model with its American counterpart. Or as Ross puts it so well, schools in the program seek "to blend the rigorous standards of learning that are characteristic of the French educational system with American approaches that value individuality and critical thinking."

Perhaps I might be permitted here to evoke a personal memory. My wife and I had an opportunity to visit one of the first classes to open through the French Heritage Language Program, and we were struck by the agility the students showed in passing from one language to the other with obvious pleasure, as if it were a game. I remember as well a parent of one of the students, a Haitian taxi driver, and how proud he was to see his son getting along so well in English, while at the same time improving in his native French.

This is why we must hope that this book finds attentive readers on both sides of the Atlantic and even beyond, for this kind of school, which is contributing to a revolution in bilingual education, is one of the effective means of fighting against closemindedness which generates intolerance and violence. In the immediate aftermath of the French Ministry of National Education's promulgation, in August 2019, of a decree encouraging foreign organizations to develop a new category of schools in France, the *établissements publics locaux d'enseignement international* (EPLEI: local public establishments of international education), no one can doubt that Ross's analysis, despite the differences in context, has the potential to lead the way. Ross shows that, far from weakening students' feeling of national belonging, this kind of school on the contrary reinforces it, while at the same time preparing them to meet the demands of dialogue between cultures.

—Philippe Joutard
Paris, France - October 2019
Translated by Christopher Caines

Acknowledgments

I am grateful for the support and encouragement of many individuals who generously shared their time and knowledge, and who also offered both assistance and encouragement.

Professor Philip Hosay served as my mentor and advisor throughout my doctoral work at NYU, directing my studies and helping to identify key issues for productive research. Committee members Dr. James Fraser and Dr. Herrick Chapman provided wisdom and direction as I explored both French history and the history of education in the United States. Dr. Dana Burde and Dr. Rene Arcilla offered encouragement and advice through the final stages of proposal writing and offered their time and energy to participating as outside readers in my defense.

I would also like to thank the many other colleagues, friends, and family members whose participation in my research was invaluable and enormously appreciated: Professor Philip Joutard and Genevieve Joutard followed my research from its inception, offering valuable insights, introductions, and perspectives; Joel and Denise Vallat shared their own experiences in New York and in France.

Appreciation is also extended to the many members of the Lycée's extended network of alumni, trustees, faculty and parents who provided their insights in surveys and interviews, and especially to Sean Lynch, Stephan Haimo, Joelle Reilly, Robert Pine, Mira Schor, and Professor Marestella Lorch, Don Zivcovich, Michele Moss, and Jean Marie Guehenno.

Appreciation is also warmly expressed to Dr. Fabrice Jaumont who has followed and shared in this effort from the beginning, and special thanks go to Jack Klempay for his meticulous assistance.

Table of Contents

CHAPTER I

Introduction

My connection to France and to the French language began when I was about ten years old. My father surprised my mother with an extraordinary Christmas gift: a portrait of her paternal grandmother, Mary Chapeze that he was able to retrieve from a family estate in Tennessee and ship to our home in Connecticut. It had occupied a place of honor in my mother's home as she was growing up, and then was ensconced above our mantel in Connecticut throughout my childhood. The portrait was finely painted by an itinerant artist in Kentucky in the middle of the 19th century, when Mary Chapeze was probably in her late teens. My mother had only met her once, when she was four and her grandmother in her late eighties, but she was a link to an earlier generation and to family history that my mother had been told included a Huguenot ancestor who had come to America with Lafayette.

With little concrete evidence beyond the portrait, my mother pursued the story of this French ancestor, gradually uncovering clues through correspondence with distant relatives and later through genealogy websites and finally an extended trip to archives in France. We learned that the great grandfather of Mary Chapeze, Dr. Henri Chapiers of Nevers, France, had indeed enlisted to sail with Lafayette as a mere 14-year-old boy. He was possibly a Protestant, was able to read and write, and apparently, as the son of a midwife, also had enough medical training that despite his young age, he joined Lafayette's regiment as a surgeon. His name was eventually changed to Henry Chapeze. His story was dramatically summed up in an 1897 biography of his son Benjamin:

> His father was Dr. Henry Chapeze, a native of France, who, imbued with the spirit and love of liberty, came to America with the Marquis de La Fayette and offered his sword and his talents to the colonies in their struggle for independence; he served as a surgeon in the American army.

I was naturally enchanted by this image of my French ancestor, who chose to remain in America, settling in (along with many other soldiers who accompanied Lafayette) in the then territory of Kentucky shortly before it was admitted as the fifteenth state. There were many unanswered questions I would have loved to ask him, however, and not enough documents telling the stories of his life. I wondered, for example, how he learned English; perhaps from the Irish girl in New York whom he married but later divorced? Did he ever consider returning to France? Did he speak French with his two sons? His home and office eventually became a local landmark in Bardstown Kentucky, where he settled. Over the years when it served as a hotel, restaurant, and sometimes both, he was often referred to as the "eminent French Doctor from Paris" (although there is no indication of any Parisian connection), but clearly he maintained a French identity even though he never returned. Would he have sent his sons to a French school had one been available to them?

As I began to consider writing this book, after more than 30 years teaching in a French school and working with French educators, I thought often about what it means to be French when connections to France are distant, either in time or in space. As I explored the network of French schools abroad, including the one where I enjoyed a long and rewarding career, I came to understand that not only were individual family connections to France fostered in these schools, but also that the French nation itself and its governments through the years, took an active role in providing this French education so that families could retain their "Frenchness". Extending beyond the goals of French families, France also promotes the French language and French culture by supporting these schools and opening them to a large international community. My French ancestor could hardly have imagined the opportunities to be both French and American that would open up during the two centuries following his arrival in the wilderness territory of Kentucky. In fact, the French government has increasingly supported both French schools abroad and the teaching of French internationally.

In the fall of 2017, French President Emmanuel Macron addressed a group of students in Ouagadougou, the capital of Burkina Faso during his first visit to Africa since taking office the previous spring. The tour, beginning in Burkina Faso and including Ghana as well as another former French colony, the Ivory Coast, was designed to present Macron's vision for Africa and to address ongoing issues on the continent, including efforts to reduce migration, combat terrorism and support human rights. But Macron also used the occasion to announce his pledge to make the French language the first language of Africa, and perhaps of the world.[1]

Earlier in the speech, referring to the many variations of French spoken throughout the Francophone countries of the world, Macron insisted on the universality of the French language as the "cement" that binds the Francophone countries together:

> For a long time, the French language, our language, has not been only French. It has spread throughout the world and it is what binds us together. We are lucky to have our language and our language has a future… especially in Africa. The future [of French], its influence, its attractiveness does not belong to France. Francophonie is a living body, a body that extends beyond our borders with a heart that beats not far from here.[2]

Macron's pledge that French become "the most spoken language in the world" was echoed earlier in 2017 when he attended an inaugural event at the City University of New York to launch a fund to support French dual language programs in public schools (initially $1.4 million and expected to grow to over $2 million).

Expanding press coverage both in the United States and in France noted the increase in the popularity of French, French dual language programs, and bilingual immersion programs. For example, the French language was surprisingly newsworthy in the United States during the early months of 2014. The *New York Times* featured the "Bilingual Revolution" taking place in New York City's public schools in response to increasing demand for French bilingual and dual language programs, noting in particular the support for these programs by the French government.[3] This article elicited a response from conservative columnist John McWhorter in a *New Republic* article, "Let's Stop Pretending That French Is an Important Language"[4], matched in turn by expanded press coverage both in the

United States and in France proclaiming the popularity of French, French dual language programs, and support for bilingual education in general. *Forbes Magazine* featured a report commissioned by the French banking group Natixis estimating that by the year 2050, French will be the most spoken language in the world, with over 750 million French speakers, outpacing both English and Mandarin Chinese. Even while questioning the Natixis study, Forbes proclaimed French to be "a fast-growing, global language" and one that "will be present on all continents and particularly predominant in a continent that, by 2050, should be a fast-growing economic powerhouse–Africa."[5]

The Globalization of Education

The growth of French language programs also intersects a growing trend towards internationalization and globalization in education, both at the level of higher education and in primary and secondary schools. Recent promotional material for Avenues, a for-profit private school that opened in New York City in 2013, is representative of this trend: "If 'local' schools are the first step in the evolution of schooling and 'national' schools are the second step, the decades ahead are likely to bring the third step. *global schools.*"[6]

This recent emphasis on global education and the expansion or internationalization of institutions such as New York University (to Abu Dhabi and Shanghai) and Yale University (to Singapore) are creating new models for the globalization of higher education. These reach beyond earlier models of study abroad and student exchange programs to establish global institutions. Other educational businesses, including Edison Schools and Global Educational Management Systems (GEMS), operate schools in the United States, the United Kingdom, the Middle East and India, and are models for further expansion of "global" schools. Additionally, beginning in 1968, the International Baccalaureate Program, a non-profit organization based in Geneva, Switzerland, has offered a curriculum and diploma program that has been adopted by over 4,000 schools internationally. Even the controversial Turkish cleric, Fethullah Gülen, has established an international network of schools, including over 150 charter schools in the United States.

This globalization of schooling has become a lively focus for research in the field of international education; however, few scholars have looked at specific model "global" schools. My study of the history of French schools outside of France, and specifically French schools in New York, proposes that the network of over 490 French schools in 130 countries constitutes a fruitful field of research into globalization in practice in elementary and secondary education. A case study of the Lycée Français de New York (1935 – present) and other French schools in New York explores how the French national education system functions not only beyond the hexagon of France itself, but also beyond the strictly colonial "civilizing mission" that was advanced by French schools in both French colonies and former colonies. The history of these New York schools, dating back to the early nineteenth century, also provides insights into French cultural diplomacy and the changing nature of Franco-American relations through the nineteenth, twentieth, and twenty-first centuries.

Why Study French Schools in New York?

There exists a significant body of scholarship concerning France's national education system. Historians and sociologists such as Eugene Weber (1976), Rogers Brubaker (1996) and Patrick Weil (2005) are prominent in the debates linking the French national education system to issues of citizenship and identity. Weber's own seminal study notes the importance of this centralizing institution in the transformation of "peasants into Frenchmen" in the nineteenth and early twentieth centuries. Additional researchers have examined the links between citizenship and identity forged in the French schools of the colonial empire. Alice Conklin (1997), Emmanuelle Saada (2007) and Frederick Cooper (2014) have explored the role of French schools in the colonial empires of Africa and Southeast Asia, schools which served both colonizers and colonial populations in different ways. The challenges of decolonization and the integration of former colonial subjects into the national education system has also been a lively subject of recent scholarship, including work by John Bowen (2008), Stéphane Beaud (2002), Gérard Noiriel (1998), and Patrick Weil (2005) addressing controversies about headscarves, cultural challenges to France's principle of secular education and the difficulties posed by the increasingly diverse student body in France.

A gap nonetheless exists in these various historical studies of the French national education system because there are few studies of the French schools abroad that do not focus primarily on colonial and post-colonial institutions. The current network of over 490 French Schools abroad includes some that have continuously offered French curricula for almost 300 years, such as the French school of Berlin, which was founded in 1670. Many of these schools, including those in New York, Moscow, London, Berlin and Madrid, have been sustained over time by expatriates, refugees, non-French diplomats and many local non-French families who have chosen French and the French national curricula for their children. Some schools have benefited from extensive government support from Paris, others have only local support, but all have continued to offer the French national curriculum and diplomas, even in times of war when connections to France and the French government were fragile or even in some cases hostile. These schools have also shared a dual mission of providing French education to French expatriates while also educating international and local elites, thereby promoting the use of the French language and interest in French culture abroad. This important mission of cultural diplomacy emphasizes the French belief that French is a uniquely universal language and that French values are also universal values. While the schools serve expatriates for whom it is important that French children receive a French education, French schools abroad also promote "universalism" to offer elite populations abroad who embrace the education provided in these schools. As a nation of immigrants, the United States, and New York in particular, often embraces cosmopolitanism of the type offered through the French schools that are established there.

By focusing primarily on the Lycée Français de New York, this study offers insights in two additional areas. Scholars including Whitney Walton (2009), Raymonde Carroll (1990) and Philippe Roger (2005) have explored some of the complexities of French-American intercultural communications in their studies of French American education exchanges and of French anti-Americanism. My interviews with a range of alumni, families, students, and administrators of French schools in New York over several generations explores the experiences of "cultural internationalism" as French, American and other nationalities live and work together in these schools. Access to French education outside of France plays an important part in making those French children who are living abroad true French citizens, while at the same time promoting an international culture among the schools' diverse populations.

Finally, the past decade has witnessed a proliferation of scholarship in the field of heritage languages (languages other than English spoken at home), dual language, and bilingual programs in the United States. For researchers and practitioners in this field who are in search of models for such programs, the Lycée Français de New York, which has served French expatriates as well as American students and families of many different nationalities, along with the other French schools in New York, may serve as useful examples.

In summary, my research examines the exceptional extent of France's support for the education of its citizens abroad, as well as the degree to which French schools also serve as an arm of French cultural diplomacy, thus addressing gaps in both the current literature on French education and national citizenship as well as the role of primary and secondary schools in public diplomacy and foreign policy. This research will also be of interest to an expanding community of scholars addressing the sustainability and institutionalization of bilingual and heritage language programs in the United State, including Peyton et al. (2001), Olga Kagan and Maria Carriera (2011), Ofelia García et al. (2017). The research will explore what is distinctive about a school that responds to the mission of French universalism and French cultural diplomacy.

Combining interviews and surveys, and making use of archival research, I examine how these schools that serve a diverse international population advance a French national civic identity while also promoting the French language and culture abroad. After consulting the archives of the French Ministry of National Education (Ministère de l'Éducation nationale), the Ministry of Foreign Affairs (Ministère des affaires étrangères) as well as documents from the schools (newsletters and newspapers, yearbooks and other school records), I hope to contribute to broader research on the promotion of national interests and identity though education, while also considering how schools with an international student body attempt to create global citizens and promote universal values. My research will address the questions of how a curriculum specifically designed to foster national identity successfully can adapt to local conditions abroad, as well as whether such schools are capable of promoting global citizenship and French identity simultaneously. It is especially interesting to see how New York, a very cosmopolitan city, has been a site for not only this French school, but also a number of others.

Many Questions

As I began my research, I thought often of my French ancestor, Dr. Chapeze, and the kinds of questions I wish I could have asked him. Even though he never returned to France after joining Lafayette's regiment in America and eventually settling with his family in Kentucky, he clearly remained French. At the time, there were in fact many other Frenchmen in America, and many Americans who valued the French Language and mastered it in schools and universities. There were even French schools, as I would discover, in New York, the city where Henry Chapeze met his wife and where his sons were born. However, not only was it clearly impossible for me to ask him directly about his French identity, he also did not leave behind written documents that I could consult. Searching for more accessible sources, I looked into my own career of over 30 years as a teacher in a French School in New York, the Lycée Français of New York, and began to formulate the kinds of questions that could help me understand not only the ways in which families sustain French identities even when far from France, but also the ways in which the French government helps support these efforts.

Eventually, I was able to craft a primary research question concerning how French K-12 schools abroad, and specifically the Lycée Français de New York, support a dual mission: serving a broader mission of French cultural diplomacy within the context of New York City's cosmopolitan culture while also supporting French expatriates living abroad so that they can return to France someday. The *mission civilisatrice* (translated into English as the "civilizing mission") famously served as the rationale for France's colonial ambitions in Africa and Asia, promoting the belief that France would spread the ideals of western civilization to native populations who would benefit from these efforts to modernize and spread the republican ideals of French democracy and education. [7] This rationale would seem inappropriate in the context of French schools in a place like New York, which was never part of the French Empire. However, I argue that the mission of promoting French culture and ideals internationally has also been an essential role for these schools which serve not only French citizens who live abroad for varied reasons, but also local non-French families in cosmopolitan areas, as well as expatriates among the elites of both diplomatic and business communities. This mission of cultural diplomacy or "soft power" is one that the French government acknowledges as essential to maintaining France's status as a world power. However, it is also a mission that is directed not only by government agencies (notably the Ministry of Foreign Affairs) but which also has a life of its own, promoted both intentionally and even at times unknowingly by French citizens and their Francophile allies throughout the world.

CHAPTER II

The Creation of the French School
at Home & Abroad

When Henry Chapeze left France in about 1776 to join Lafayette's regiment and sail for America, he would have been one of the fewer than fifteen percent of the greater French population who spoke the French language, rather than one of the many regional languages of Provence, Alsace, Brittany, Normandy and other provinces. His mother, a mid-wife, was able to read and write, although his father, a builder of wine casks, was not. We do not know if Henry attended any of the schools that were gradually expanding throughout France in the years before the French Revolution, but like his mother, he could read and write, and perhaps his skills as a physician were acquired from her, as there would not have been any formal medical school training in Nevers for him. As I began to consider the role of French schools abroad, and the unique manner in which France supports and promotes its national education system overseas, I needed to begin by understanding the role that a national education system played in the centralization of the French State itself.

Schools have been the key instruments in the creation of French citizenship since the time of the French Revolution. In addition, the French language itself and French high culture (especially art and literature) were part of broad efforts of French cultural diplomacy since the time of the Ancien Regime, beginning with Francois I and the creation of the Franco-Turkish alliance in 1536. As a result, the sultan Suleiman the Magnificent granted special status to the French language and to French culture more generally in the Ottoman Empire that was to endure for over two centuries. Similarly, Louis XIII assured the status of French in Canada, Madagascar, Tunis and Algiers and later throughout the Far East through the Foreign Missionary Society in Paris (Société des missions étrangères de Paris).[8] This chapter will examine the important place held by the

French language in French notions of citizenship since the eighteenth century, before turning to the early history of the promotion of French language and French culture abroad, especially in the nineteenth and early twentieth centuries. An important part of this story is the French Lay Mission (Mission laïque française or MLF), which was the first systematic attempt to create a network of secular French schools abroad with programs aligned to the national French curriculum.

Rousseau and Herder: Education and Citizenship

The key to understanding how a national school system functions outside its national borders is understanding the function of the school system as a part of the development of a nation itself. In both the United States and France, the concept of political nationalism, as distinct from cultural nationalism helped to shape the manner in which schools educated future citizens.

The philosophical roots of this emphasis on education and citizenship can be traced to the European Enlightenment of the late eighteenth century when, as Susanne Wiborg points out, "the notion of education as being a useful tool for developing a common national identity within specific geographical borders arose." [9] Two philosophers in particular developed two distinct theories that informed this new understanding of the role of education and schools in societies where education previously "functioned primarily as a vehicle for fulfilling an ecclesiastical need" and was related more towards training clergy than towards developing citizens.[10]

The theory of the social contract, developed by Jean-Jacques Rousseau (1712 – 1778), formed the basis for a concept of political nationalism and for an educational system that could create citizens and patriots, and eventually a better society. For Rousseau, a system of public education, provided by the state, was an essential function of government:

> There can be no patriotism without liberty, no liberty without virtue, no virtue without citizens; create citizens and you have everything you need; without them, you have nothing but debased slaves, from rulers of the State downwards. To

form citizens is not the work of the day; and in order to have men it is necessary to educate them when they are children.[11]

Rousseau's arguments in favor of civic education were aimed both towards supporting the idea of government institutions as "instruments by which the national character can be fashioned and a love of country inspired,"[12] and as an argument against the functions of religious education during the 1750s and 1760s. Rousseau's support of the secular functions of education, serving the development of moral, ethical and political virtues of citizenship rather than the functions of the church, thus also formed the basis of what would become the French national education system.

Rousseau also addressed the manner in which children should be educated. His two works on education, *Émile ou de l'éducation* (*Émile*) and *Sur le gouvernement de la Pologne et sur sa réformation projetée* (*Consideration on the Polish Government*) include chapters on what should constitute patriotic education, emphasizing, for example, specific national identity. His recommendations for Polish schools included the following:

> At twenty, a Pole ought not to be a man of any other sort; he ought to be a Pole. I wish that, when he learns to read, he should read about his own land; that at the age of ten he should be familiar with all its products, at twelve with all its provinces, highways, and towns; that at fifteen he should know its whole history, at sixteen all its laws; that in all Poland there should be no great action or famous man of which his heart and memory are not full, and of which he cannot give an account at a moment's notice. From this you can see that it is not studies of the usual sort, directed by foreigners and priests, that I would like to have children pursue... They ought to have only Poles for teachers.[13]

This notion of a national education system certainly helps to explain the manner in which French émigrés who settled in the United States transported with them French textbooks and eventually established French schools, and is clearly reflected current in government policies that continue to guarantee a French education to all French children, wherever they might reside. This is especially the case for

French expatriates with intentions of eventually returning to France, a theme that will be explored in greater detail in the chapters that follow.

In Germany, Johann Gottfried Herder (1744 – 1803) also developed theories of education related to nation building, but with a decidedly different perspective. Drawing from German Romanticism, Herder's concept of cultural nationalism argues that national identity cannot be created as Rousseau had proposed, whether by a social contract or government intervention. Rather, Herder believes that nationalism evolves as a fundamental expression of the natural culture. Language plays a key role in both visions of national identity. For Rousseau, a national language can (and should) be acquired through education, even for citizens who perhaps do not share a "mother tongue." For Herder, on the other hand, the "mother tongue" is a primary expression of identity. Human beings form nations from common historical traditions, grounded in language, because, for Herder, the nation exists as an organic cultural community, and government itself should only (perhaps invisibly) help to reinforce the bonds that have already been forged through common history, language and culture. Education, according to Herder, then, is a "vehicle to effect the transmission of a cultural heritage from one generation to the next."[14]

In effect, the visions of Herder and Rousseau for schools are not mutually exclusive, and both served to inform the creation of national school systems in Europe throughout the nineteenth century, serving as the basis for the national systems in France and Prussia which themselves served as models for the development of public schools in the United States. The leaders of the Common School movement in New York sought to develop a national curriculum in America with recommendations for the improvement of schools based on the Prussian and French systems, as testified by a series of reports presented in 1892 to the New York State Department of Public Instruction.[15] The fact that an American commission travelled through Europe to produce these reports demonstrates the enormous influence that these national systems of education had on the development of public education in the United States.

These different perspectives also lie at the heart of different views of the rights of citizenship, complicated by the demographic necessities of nineteenth century France. As Roger Brubaker has pointed out, "the policies and politics of citizenship are strikingly different in France and Germany." [16] The former, originating in Rousseau's political nationalism granted citizenship under the policy of *jus soli*, a concept that made room for making French citizens of diverse populations within the hexagon and beyond. The German (Prussian) model of *jus sanguinis,* on the other hand, determined citizenship by cultural heritage or "blood ties." Over the centuries, thanks to what Brubaker refers to as "the ethnic strand in French self-understanding," the universalistic ideals of French citizenship have continued to play a major role in shaping French educational policy, sometimes in surprisingly and seemingly contradictory ways. For example, the strict insistence on the secular nature of public education in France has led to major confrontations over the prohibition against the wearing of headscarves by Muslim girls.

Language Centralization in France: Transforming "Peasants into Frenchmen"

The strong identification of the French language with French identity is the deliberate product of over two centuries of French nation-building as well as the efforts of French colonialism. One of the first phases of the creation of the modern nation states was the unification of peoples around a common language. While Herder proposed this as a natural evolution of the unification of people with a common language and culture in Germany, in France unification around a common language happened as a matter of deliberate government policy that closely linked education to political ideals, in spite of the initial lack of a common language.

The process of linguistic unification in France began in tandem with the policies of administrative centralization, notably with the reign of Louis XI (1461 – 1483) and later with the Edict of Villers-Cotterêts (1539), which established the supremacy of French over Latin and, importantly, over local dialects as the official language of government administration. Also, in 1539, Robert Estienne published his *Dictionaire françois-latin*, the first printed lexicon in which entries appeared in French, followed by their Latin equivalents. Historian Terence Wooldridge observes that this dictionary, "produced to help young French scholars learn classical Latin, had the simultaneous effect of promoting the mastery of French."[17] France was also increasingly unified by the close alliance between the monarchy and the Catholic Church, which although challenged briefly by the Protestant Reformation and the Edict of Nantes in 1598, was an essential feature of French national identity until the Revolution.[18] The Reformation, with its emphasis on written material as a means to disseminate Protestant ideas throughout Europe, saw the expanding influence of the printing press, and so also helped to promote French as a national language.

This gradual process of linguistic unification ultimately led to the creation of the French Academy (Académie française) in 1635 by Cardinal Richelieu as a state-sanctioned guardian of the national language. Richelieu would also help to ensure the rise of French as an important international language. The Academy established a single standard national language with rules of rhetoric and grammar as well as spelling. Louis XIV authorized the publication of a single national dictionary in 1673, a date that according to some, lives in infamy for the millions of French school children who have been "martyrs of spelling" ever since: "All of the children who suffer today to learn French spelling can curse the day of Monday, 8 May 1673, the dark day when the *académiciens* made the decision to adopt a standard spelling, at first only for themselves but which they would later force upon the general public."[19]

Despite these efforts, French remained the language of less than 15% of the country's population in the years leading up to the Revolution. The French Revolution itself also became a unifying force, as Sue Wright notes in her work on the role of language in nation – state building and European integration: "Linguistic unification was seen as a prime requirement in a participatory political system which derived its legitimacy from the people and which would not be achieved unless the revolutionaries could create a community of communication."[20] Interestingly, the first language census of France conducted after the Revolution indicated that as few as 3 million out of a population of 25 million French citizens spoke French as a "mother tongue."[21]

Citing the French sociologist Pierre Bourdieu, linguist Harold Schiffman argues that "until the French Revolution, the process of linguistic unification was indistinguishable from the process of the construction of the monarchical state," and the effort to expand the revolution itself gave a new impetus for "forging a common language"[22]. "The imposition of the legitimate language against the *idioms* and *patois* is part of the political strategies destined to assure the perpetuation of the gains of the Revolution by the production and reproduction of the new man."[23] Another important figure in this respect was the French philosopher and political scientist the Marquis de Condorcet (1743 – 1794), who saw the role that education, along with language, played in the shaping of the republican subject. According to Philippe Joutard, a noted French historian and the former rector of the academies of Besançon and Toulouse, Condorcet believed that "the universal Man, the modern French citizen, should be educated by a network of schools dependent on the state," an idea which continues to shape French educational policy at home and abroad to this day.[24]

With the Revolution, the French language itself became the standard bearer not only of the nation, but also of the philosophical and political underpinnings of the nation. The French language, deemed to be the embodiment of rational modern democracy, became a unifying feature of the Revolution so that citizenship and language became joined in a national education system that helped to spread French to a variety of geographically linked populations, which previously spoke entirely separate languages—including Alsace in the east, Brittany in the northwest, Occitan, Provence, and Basque in the south, among others. As Joutard explains, "From the very beginning, the role of schools in France has been to build unity, and in particular to reduce regional differences. French education takes people from Britany, from Corsica, from Provence and tries to make them French."[25] In this sense it can be said that the French education system fosters a strongly unitary conception of what it means to be French, one which is built around the nation and its republican values, and which erases regional differences. Similarly, historian Mitchel Lasser explains that the French education system is "the key institution in the construction, maintenance, and dissemination of this dominant ideology of the unified and republican bases of the French citizenry and of the French state" and that the French education system "constitutes the primary vector for the transmission and reproduction of French cultural understanding," a fact that has been noted by many leading French intellectuals from Louis Althusser to Pierre Bourdieu.[26]

However, the transition from regional dialects to French was rarely easy or peaceful. Olivier Boasson, the former Deputy Cultural Councilor of the French Embassy to the United States and the former Deputy Director General of the Agency for French Education Abroad (Agence pour l'enseignement français à l'étranger), explains that the imposition of the French language throughout France was a traumatic process for speakers of regional languages: "[the imposition of French] was very painful and it involved a lot of political force and brutality, and it did a lot of harm to regional languages."[27] As internal migrants moved from the countryside to urban centers, especially Paris, they also moved from regional languages and dialects to a standardized form of French. Throughout the nineteenth century, French thus increasingly displaced regional languages through the combined effects of internal migration and an expanding network of school teachers, who were themselves often forced to migrate from home villages to teach elsewhere, and through the military service, which also bonded disparate regional language speakers through the commonality of French.[28] Simply put, "the idea [was] to define national unity in terms of linguistic unity"[29] or, in the language of Weber, to transform "peasants into Frenchmen."

The Role of the Ministry of National Education

From its creation in 1808, the French Ministry of National Education (Ministère de l'Éducation nationale) has been the central institution responsible for socializing children into their roles as French citizens in a national society beyond their immediate families, towns and villages. In France, this critical role was recognized as early as 1816, when royal ordinances established standards of competence for teaching, and were followed in 1833 with laws initiated by Francois Guizot, the Minister of Public Instruction, which required that communes set up and maintain public schools and establish a system of inspectors to monitor quality.[30] According to the education historian Charles Glenn, "Substituting a national language for the local dialects of indigenous regional groups was a major motivation in the development of state sponsored schooling over the course of the late eighteenth and nineteenth centuries in Europe."[31] Similarly, Joutard sees Guizot as an intermediary link between Condorcet and the public education system initiated by the Jules Ferry laws under the Third Republic, in the sense that he was the first to mandate a nationwide primary school system in France.[32]

By 1847 France had over 60,000 schools attended by over 3.5 million children. Quality varied greatly, education for girls lagged behind, and clandestine schools where instruction continued in regional languages still operated. The greatest change, however, came in 1881 and 1882 when the reforms introduced by Jules Ferry abolished all school fees and made enrollment in public or private schools compulsory. As Weber has noted, one of the greatest challenges this new school system faced was the fact that even in the latter part of the nineteenth century, a substantial part of the adult population of France, (and therefore their children) did not speak French. The solution Weber describes was simple: "Officially, the problem was faced by denying its existence."[33] Even the definition of "mother tongue" was adapted to suit the process of making French the sole national language. A French military examination manual from 1875, for example, explains:

> (1) We call mother tongue the tongue that is spoken by our parents, and in particular our mothers; spoken also by our fellow citizens and the persons who inhabit the same country as us.
>
> (2) Our mother tongue is French.[34]

Thus, the first waves of internal migrants in France, the teachers, soldiers and rural inhabitants who moved to urban centers were often intimately involved in the Republican school system that sought to make them French citizens not only through civic education, but primarily through the French language, usually at the expense of regional languages and cultures. Punishment for children caught speaking native languages other than French was routine, and often combined with the humiliation of regional customs. For example, a child caught speaking Breton would be obliged to carry a *sabot* (wooden shoe, a symbol of rural peasantry) until he could catch a classmate committing the same crime and so pass the shoe on to the next humiliated victim.[35]

Weber maintains that the successful propagation of French was due to the combined effects of compulsory military service, expanded kindergartens and compulsory education for girls who, as future mothers, could pass the language to their children. Additionally, the national system of education created a national network of public employees, including teachers, and an expanded apparatus of government service which itself created employment opportunities while also reinforcing national identity and loyalty. One French civics text, for example, explained that a good primary education was a path to a good, secure job in government service. The stakes for a strong national education system were raised even higher following the national humiliation of France after its defeat during the Franco-Prussian War (1870 – 1871). Indeed, some military historians have attributed France's defeat to the weakness of France's military education system as opposed to Prussia's.[36]

This same period, the dawn of the Third Republic, saw the vast expansion of French colonial apparatus, and thus even greater employment opportunities in government service. The powerful history textbook written for use in primary schools by Ernest Lavisse in 1884 also helped communicate notions of citizenship and identity, so much so that historian Pierre Nora features both the Lavisse text and the classic *Tour de France par deux enfants* as "sites of memory" in his landmark study of French history and culture.[37] By the end of the nineteenth century, Émile Durkheim was able to declare in his *Rules of Sociological Method* that education was the primary means through which the individual was socialized; in short, it is Durkheim's view that "French schools interpret and express the French spirit."[38]

French Schools in the Colonies

If the Ferry laws and the construction of the national education system in France served to transform "peasants into Frenchmen," the French school system abroad, especially in the colonial empire, also sought to extend the French language, culture, and in some cases, citizenship beyond the borders of the French hexagon. The impact of the Napoleonic wars and the creation of multi-national, overseas French military forces proved to be the ultimate "linguistic melting pot" and also provided the impetus for the extraordinary expansion of the French national education system throughout the world. This expansion was designed to meet the needs of soldiers and officers (not to mention at least some colonial subjects) ensuring the spread of the French national education system (and therefore French identity) throughout the empire and beyond.[39]

The administration of French schools in the colonies began with the underlying assumption that the imposition of the French language itself would play a substantial role in transmitting loyalty and identity, molding at least some of the indigenous populations into potential Frenchmen while also serving the colonial administrators and their families. In some cases, education in the French language helped identify those indigenous students most likely to become *évolués* (more advanced) and helpful to the French administration. In others, it was a simple expedient for colonial administrators faced with a plethora of indigenous languages they could not have mastered. One of the major benefits of the extensive network of French schools in the colonies was that it meant there was no general need for colonial administrators to learn the local languages. Similarly, French public schools in the colonies did not routinely include courses in indigenous languages, leaving much of that instruction, where it existed at all, to native, often religious schools. For example, Arabic was not even an official language in Algeria until 1947, and even then, there was a chronic shortage of teachers, so instruction was limited.[40]

The decision to make French the language of instruction in colonial schools reflects both universalistic and assimilationist goals of the *mission civilisatrice* ("civilizing mission"), a nineteenth- and twentieth-century rationalization of colonization based on the idea that France and other European countries were spreading Western civilization to the indigenous peoples of Africa, Asia, and the Americas. As the historian William Fortescue puts it, at the time "it was widely believed that French civilization was superior to all other contemporary civilizations, that the values of French civilization were potentially universal and that the French had a special mission to spread their civilization throughout the world."[41]

Education was to play a central role in this mission, although it was to be an education built upon a highly racialized and paternalistic model. Jules Ferry—who was almost singlehandedly responsible for the institutionalization and standardization of France's public education system—was also one of France's most ardent advocates of colonialism. In a speech to the National Assembly on July 28, 1885, Ferry made the following declaration: "I repeat that the superior races have a right, because they have a duty. They have a duty to civilize the inferior races."[42] As these words attest, the use of French in French schools abroad would be an expedient for colonial administrators, especially in Africa where, as Alice Conklin observes, "there were simply too many African dialects to master," but also because the imagined values of the French language would be crucial to helping the colonized "make the leap from barbarism to civilization."[43]

Although European missionaries were generally the first to create schools in both French and in British colonies in Africa, the French government brought these schools under direct control of Paris through a series of laws between 1902 and 1924 that, combined with the strict policies of secularization in effect both in France and abroad, limited aid to missionary schools, which eventually accounted for only a small percentage of schools abroad. According to social anthropologist Bob W. White, the British approach was considerably more "laissez-faire," with the British government granting much greater autonomy to the missionary societies' schools: "Britain's laissez-faire attitude towards missions in the colonies relieved it of the responsibility of educational administration and policy formation which the French assumed in their colonies before the turn of the century."[44] Even when the British colonial administration took a more active role in overseeing education in the colonies, missionary schools continued to dominate, and the use of local languages was encouraged especially in primary schools.

The French Lay Mission

Although the French Lay Mission (Mission laïque française or MLF) grew out of civil society and is based on the premise of its independence from the French government, it represents one of the first instances where the desire to promote and monitor French education abroad led to the creation of a secular organization officially linked to the French government and fully dedicated to French schools abroad. A major goal was to replace the influence of the extensive network of Catholic missionary schools, as well as those that were linked to the Alliance Israelite Universelle, a Jewish organization created in 1860 to support French Schools which served primarily Jewish families in the Middle East and North Africa.

The MLF had its origins in France's colonies, specifically Madagascar. In 1898, the Governor of Madagascar, General Joseph Gallieni, began an initiative to export French education to the colony. Gallieni saw schools as one of the primary mechanisms of French colonial control: he once wrote that "roads and schools are the areas upon which we should concentrate our efforts [trans.]."[45] Gallieni was particularly interested in primary education, which he believed would accomplish two things. On the one hand, he wished to export what he saw as the universal values of the French humanist tradition. On the other, he saw the political utility of cultural education, so that the indigenous population "would become accustomed to [French] customs, language, and our way of dressing [trans.]."[46] Moreover, Gallieni believed that it was essential that French colonial schools carry out their instruction in French and according to the guidelines of the national curriculum, rather than the religious teachings of the missionary schools that had controlled the education of the local population and had been willing to carry out their instruction in Malagasy up until that point: "Madagascar has become a French territory. The French language must therefore become the language of instruction in the schools on this island [trans.]."[47] As Olivier Boasson explains, Gallieni was not the only one to hold such beliefs:

> In the nineteenth and at the beginning of the twentieth century, there was a deeply-rooted and very sincere notion that [France's] messianic calling should be accomplished through education and that colonized people should be educated and enlightened. That was a widely held idea in the nineteenth and twentieth centuries, especially among high-

ranking French officials abroad, whether in colonies or with trading partners.[48]

This "messianic calling" came to be known as the *mission civilisatrice*, and would play an important part in the early development of the network of French schools abroad, as described above.

In June of 1898, Governor Gallieni appointed Pierre Deschamps, a young literature professor and an alumnus of the École normale supérieure in Saint-Cloud, to lead the organization of the new education system on the island of Madagascar. At the time, most of the instruction of the indigenous population was carried out by missionary schools, which dispensed a religious education and usually carried out their instruction in Malagasy. Deschamps's task was to replace this network of religious schools with a secular system designed to follow the French model. It is in this setting that Deschamps developed many of the political and pedagogical principles that would later lead to the foundation of the MLF.

In the years following his return to France, Deschamps met with several influential French political figures to discuss his project for a network of secular schools in the colonies, including Pierre Forcin, the founder and secretary general of the Alliance Française.[49] The MLF itself was founded on June 8th, 1902 when a general assembly approved the first MLF charter. In 1907, the French government awarded the MLF the status of a charitable organization, allowing the MLF to expand its activities throughout the French colonies.

The creation of the MLF and its continuity would not have been possible without support of influential individuals within the French government. Although the MLF was a non-governmental organization, several members of its board of directors held important positions in the Ministry of the Interior, the Ministry of Education, the Chamber of Deputies, and other branches of the French government. The MLF has maintained a close relationship with the French government throughout its existence. In 1906, for instance, the board of the MLF included Gaston Doumergue, Vice-President of the Chamber of Deputies and Minister of Colonies, Commerce, Industry, Labor, Education and Religious Affairs, as well as B. Baudrillard, the national inspector of elementary schools.

Other notable early board members included Camille Bloch (national inspector of libraries and archives), Fernand Dubief (deputy and former Minister of the Interior, Commerce, Industry, Post and Telegraph), M. Blanchier (a senator from Charente), and J.-B. Bienvenu-Martin (a senator and the Minister of Justice, Education, Labor and Religious Affairs).[50] The MLF also received significant financial and political support from the French Ministry of National Education. For example, in 1905 the MLF received 60,000 francs from the French state to support its overseas educational activities. Following the official separation of church and state in that same year, the French state signed an agreement with the MLF agreeing to disburse at least 18,000 francs per year to the organization over a period of 20 years. As historian Randi Deguilhem puts it, "in an ideological as well as a financial way, the MLF may, especially during the colonial period, be considered almost an overseas branch of the French Ministry of Education."[51] The MLF was also closely linked to the French public-school system, and many of its members were public school teachers or administrators.[52]

The primary purpose of the MLF was to create a network of secular schools on the French model for the local students living in French colonies or in other parts of the world where France exerted its political and cultural influence, or otherwise had an economic presence. In other words, the goal of the MLF can be summarized as follows: to propagate secular education abroad, following the French model, while taking into account the differing cultural contexts in host countries. For this reason, the MLF's work focused primarily on the Middle East and reached beyond the borders of the colonial empire: between 1905 and 1910, it spearheaded the creation of Lycées in Thessaloniki (Greece) and Beirut (Lebanon), as well as in Cairo and Alexandria (Egypt). It pursued its work in the region after World War I, especially in Syria and Egypt and after World War II in Libya and Sudan.

Broadly speaking, the MLF had two major objectives. Firstly, the MLF sought to provide an alternative to the network of primary and secondary schools which had been established in French colonies by the Roman Catholic Church and the Israelite Mission. These schools were run by Catholic missionaries and by Jewish societies and sought to provide a religious education to local populations, rather than the strictly secular education that was obligatory in the French public-school system by that time. Deschamps firmly believed that a secular education on the French model should be made available to every child in the colonies, regardless of their race or national origin. He infused the institution with the idea that local populations should have access to an education that would allow them to attain autonomy rather than impose the model of assimilation or a religious ideology. In this sense, the MLF reflected the heated debates on secularism and education that dominated French public discourse throughout the late nineteenth and early twentieth centuries, and were cemented into French law by the Jules Ferry laws in 1881 and 1882, followed by the official separation of church and state in France in 1905. [53] This issue continues to be contested even today, as demonstrated by the ongoing debates over headscarves in schools.

Secondly, the MLF sought to promote the use of French throughout the colonies, in particular as a mission of cultural diplomacy, as these schools would be vehicles for spreading French culture and civilization. This was accomplished by implementing a French program in MLF schools and by conducting most classes in French. As was the case in Gallieni's Madagascar, the MLF's promotion of French was explicitly seen as a tool to increase France's political influence abroad, particularly in its colonies. In this sense, the MLF shared the same ambition as the Alliance Française, created in 1883 to facilitate the spread of French language and culture abroad, and especially to promote French enlightenment philosophy and Republican values in the colonies. While the Alliance addressed larger cultural activities and French instruction generally (including classes for adults and cultural programs), the MLF was specifically a vehicle for creating and supporting elementary and secondary schools with a specific mission, that of exporting French Republican values:

> [The MLF exists within the context of] the radical humanist tradition that at the time defended values of the Republic against religious sects that would not accept these values of their own volition. That was the idea at the beginning: to

project the values of the Republic beyond the hexagon, while taking into account the specificities of the host countries [trans.].[54]

As the statement above makes clear, the mission of the MLF was originally articulated in terms of cultural diplomacy, and specifically in terms of the dissemination of the values of the French Republic around the world, while at the same time being willing to adapt itself to local conditions. In these ways, the MLF shared the mission of the Alliance Française, namely the "desire to spread French cultural and political influence overseas by increasing the use of the French language by non-Francophone groups."[55] This vocation is still felt today, and has had a lasting impact on French schools abroad. In several important ways, the MLF is a reflection of the idea that education is a core aspect of French identity, and that the network of schools represents an effective means to advance France's cultural influence, status, and prestige throughout the world.

The creation at the beginning of the twentieth century of the MLF can therefore been seen as part of an effort to spread France's Republican ideals throughout the world, especially around the Mediterranean and especially in the Middle East, areas of the world in which France had a strong colonial presence, a project which continues to this day. However, the MLF realized this vision using means particular to its educational mission. As explained by André Thévenin, an historian of the MLF, the organization was able to further its goal through its control over faculty, schools, and the curriculum.[56]

The story of MLF schools abroad serves as a useful model for the development of French schools in North America, even in those cases when the latter do not fall directly under the MLF's supervision. For example, the MLF opened the way for increasing adaptation of French schools abroad to local conditions while still emphasizing an underlying mission of promoting not only the French language, but also French culture and values. One example, Randi Deguilhem's study of MLF schools in Syria between 1920 and 1967 illustrates the extent to which the MLF's educational mission was linked to the cultural politics of the French state. During this period, the MLF founded three schools in Syria: in 1925, it established a school in Damascus and one in Aleppo and, in 1935, another in Tartous.[57] The stated mission of these schools was, as Deguilhem puts it, "to turn Syrians into Frenchmen." This was accomplished in large part through the imposition of a standardized curriculum based on the French model:

> Such a standardized study program throughout the MLF school network was to create a common cultural base for students attending the schools located abroad. As a result of this exposure to French culture and history, these students, aside from being eligible to sit for the French *baccalauréat* exams at the conclusion of their high school years, would have presumably cultivated an affinity or even a loyalty for things French.[58]

As such, the fate of the MLF schools in Syria was inextricably linked to colonial politics and French foreign policy. As Deguilhem writes, throughout its history MLF saw its mission as one of intellectual colonization:

> The Mission's official policy was opposed to violent imperialistic means but its methodology was to win over individuals by cultivating their intellectual prerogative of wanting to belong to French culture and civilization. Despite its pacifist approach, the MLF was really an integral part of French colonialism.[59]

The MLF was responsible for several important educational innovations, mostly in response to the need to adapt itself to local conditions. As Thévenin describes: "new teaching methods highlight the Mission's willingness to adapt itself to local conditions, as well as to the expectations of needs of local populations [trans.]."[60] One way this was reflected was by the MLF's willingness to conduct instruction in two languages, namely French and the local language (often Arabic), as well as by the decision to integrate the MLF schools into the country's education system in different ways, depending on the local conditions. For example, students at the school in Beirut took the French baccalaureate. Meanwhile, their peers in Damascus took the Syrian baccalaureate, and the school's curriculum was designed to prepare students to be admitted to the University of

Damascus. In Aleppo, the school focused on vocational training to make students competitive in the local job market.

As the network expanded, the MLF needed more and more competent teachers. For this reason, the Jules Ferry Institute was created in November 1902 in order to train future teachers for the MLF. In line with MLF associationist attitude, teachers were trained in the language of the region in which they would be teaching. Randi Deguilhem explains:

> The future teachers would be specifically trained in languages of the regions to which they were sent in order to ease potential communication obstacles with students, parents and the local administration... The Jules Ferry Institute also equipped their teachers with a practical knowledge of on-site difficulties about the country in which they were to work, such as particular agricultural hardships found there, water deficiencies and insect problems, etc.[61]

The MLF was responsible for several other important pedagogical innovations. One particularly good illustration of the MLF's willingness to adapt is the Lycée de Téhéran, which opened its doors on November 1, 1928. All classes there were taught in French, except for those having to do with the national culture of Iran. In practice, this meant that there were classes on Persian language and literature, as well as Persian history and geography, which were taught in Persian by Iranian faculty.[62] According to Besnard, this decision was made to allow the free expression of national pride, to not offend the local culture, and to ease the tensions between France and Iran that were mounting at the time. His dream was a "penetration and fusion of cultures."[63]

Of course, the decision to adapt the curriculum and language of instruction to local conditions was not uncontroversial, particularly because of the centralization of the education system of France and the universalizing impulse that characterizes French language and culture. In 1930, a debate erupted over the curriculum at the MLF school in Beirut. André Thérive, a journalist for the French daily *L'Opinion*, wrote an article denouncing the projects to adapt the curriculum to the Lebanese context. His comments are worth citing, not only for the way they illustrate the desire to centralize and standardize the curriculum of MLF schools around the world, but also because of the way they refer to the struggle between French and English for prominence on the world stage:

> I would betray my role as a teacher if I criticized the only kind of education that can turn our children into anything other than savages. And I would betray my role as a Frenchman because if we don't unify our teaching methods in every part of the world where we have an influence, if only a spiritual one, if we don't make Frenchmen in the first and the second zone, the whole world will be English.[64]

This contradiction between an expanding international network of schools and the strong centralizing and standardizing tendencies that characterize France's national education system is a theme that recurs often in the history of French education abroad. The desire to centralize is often resisted by the schools themselves, forcing administrators to adapt to local conditions. What is particularly illuminating in the comment cited above, however, is the way that the problem is framed in terms of a rivalry with global English; this is a problem which has not disappeared, and the French Ministries of Foreign Affairs and of National Education continue to be concerned about increasing competition from "global English," further emphasizing the high geopolitical and diplomatic stakes involved in France's network of schools around the world.

The Legacy of French Colonial Schools

In the post-colonial era, the role of the French language remains highly contested in some former colonies, notably in Algeria, which has implemented a policy of Arabization, which has included replacing French with English as the most favored second language in schools. Another result of this colonial legacy of the French language is a highly varied legacy of language abilities among immigrants from the former colonial empire, who today comprise a significant portion of the immigrant population within France and who, along with their children, enroll in schools in France, where only very recently has there been any effort to acknowledge their linguistic competencies.[65]

Despite this and other contestations, there still exists a very strong linguistic and cultural bond between France and its former colonies, one that is in large part maintained by the presence of French schools in these countries. Jean-Marie Guéhenno, a former Cultural Counselor of the French Embassy to the United States, explains:

> It's striking to see how decades after decolonization, all the elites of the former colonies are still very influenced by France, and they still want to go to France. [The schools] did not prevent decolonization, because that was a historical movement that was stronger than anything, but I think it did create a bond that in some ways still exists.[66]

However, it was not only within this empire that the French language and French school system developed. From the Middle East to South America to Russia, French has been highly valued as an international language of diplomacy and commerce, as well as for academic disciplines including, and especially, philosophy. Thus, almost from its creation, the national education system in France has also played a role internationally (today we might refer to the "globalization" of French education). While some have argued that linguistic and cultural imperialism are inherent in the expansion of French education and the French language overseas, others have sought to underline the "universalizing" influence of French positivist traditions in the support for French language and culture abroad.

In today's age of globalization, other languages and national systems also have developed an international reach, as witnessed by the rise of "global English" and the recent efforts by China to expand Chinese language schools internationally. [67] France, however, remains unique in its centralized and governmental support of an extensive network of overseas schools, many of which have relatively long histories, serving both expatriate French citizens and their families who may plan to return to France, and both local and international populations.

The legacy of French colonial schools is clearly evident in President Macron's speech in Ouagadougou, which celebrated the fact that French has continued to endure and spread in West Africa. However, what can the purpose of overseas schools with a national mission be in a non-colonial setting? The French schools in New York—as well as those elsewhere in the United States, Madrid, London, Moscow and Berlin—clearly have no colonial ambitions and yet they very explicitly serve government-directed missions of promoting the French language and French culture, even when the schools themselves are privately incorporated and locally directed, as is the case with the LFNY and also for its nineteenth-century predecessor, the Economical School.

One clear mission is to promote the necessary basics of a French education, especially French language, history, and geography, to allow expatriates to continue being French, whether or not they ultimately return to France, by developing their French language skills and learning the essential elements of French history. In this mission, the Lycée Français and other French schools are clearly distinguished from other private schools in New York. And unlike American schools abroad, both in France and elsewhere, these schools acquire legitimacy precisely because they are connected to the French Ministry of National Education, which assures the validation of these schools' credentials.

A further distinction is that even though these schools do not serve a colonial mission, they do a serve a mission of cultural diplomacy, and are viewed by the French government as an essential part of their diplomatic mission and their "soft power," as will be discussed in further detail in the following chapter on cultural diplomacy and the role of French schools abroad.

CHAPTER III

Cultural Diplomacy & the Role of French Schools Abroad

My first encounter with the French educational system occurred in 1971 during a Junior Year Abroad at the University of Grenoble. I was one of two Swarthmore student pioneers in this program which was sponsored by the State University of New York in Buffalo. Because a number of the Buffalo students were completing requirements for their teaching certificates, the Program partnered with one of the public high schools in Grenoble, the Lycée Stendhal, to provide the required number of "practice teaching" hours under the supervision of a certified French professor. Although I had not previously considered enrolling in a teacher training program, this seemed an ideal opportunity to immerse myself in the local context and understand more about France.

This turned out to be a fortuitous choice, when I later graduated from Swarthmore and moved to New York City. With little teaching experience other than the time spent with my French mentor at the Lycée Stendhal, it was natural that the first attempt to find a permanent job in New York was a phone call to the French Lycée, which happily was in search of an English teacher to substitute for a much-beloved, long-time teacher, who had been hospitalized unexpectedly and would not be able to return for several months.

This teacher, Mrs. Hess, who had been teaching at the school since 1947, became my second mentor. I visited her regularly in the hospital during her rehab in order to get lesson plans and keep her informed about her classes, and she shared with me her own devotion to the Lycée and its mission with remarks that have stuck with me through my career there, and certainly inspired my more recent work with the French Heritage Language Program and even the research at NYU that led to writing this book. She said that she often had friends ask why she did not choose to teach somewhere she would be "really needed" rather than at such an elite private school as the Lycée. And her response was simply that the Lycée was not only a school that served elite students, although there were many from privileged families; the school also included widely diverse families and was in fact a refuge, even for teachers and administrators, who found a home, career and comfort being part of the world-wide network of French Lycées. She also noted that these students, whether from New York, France, or much more distant places in Africa, Haiti, Australia, South America and beyond, often continued to travel and to become leaders in their own communities, so that teaching at the Lycée meant for Mrs. Hess, and for me, helping shape in some small way, an international community.

Other schools may also seek to develop a sense of international community by promoting languages or a common curriculum, but the network of French schools abroad is significantly different. Not only are they generally subsidized—either directly or indirectly—by the French government, but also, they serve two distinctive missions that most other schools, whether American or international, do not. One is to prepare students to return to France. The other—the subject of this chapter—is to serve the broader mission of French cultural diplomacy.

French Schools Abroad and Cultural Diplomacy

Unlike other private international K-12 schools, including those which offer the International Baccalaureate degree program, French schools abroad are overseen, either directly or, in the case of private schools, indirectly, by the French government, which offers its network of over 490 accredited schools around the world the possibility of recruiting fully certified French faculty and provides access to the official French national curriculum as defined by the French Ministry of National Education (Ministère de l'Éducation nationale). There are other networks of schools internationally, including most notably those which adopt the International Baccalaureate (IB) program, as well as networks of parochial schools, but these private institutions do not play a role in a national policy of cultural diplomacy. Often, they provide (for a fee) general curriculum guidelines or even, as is the case for the IB program, an entire curriculum and diploma system, adapted to different languages and national programs.

While the French schools may be unique in the degree of governmental support and interest in pre-collegiate education, they are also unique in fulfilling a governmental mission of cultural diplomacy. The French government provides financial support both to the schools directly, and also indirectly through need-based financial aid awarded to French families living abroad with school-age children. In addition to serving the needs of these French nationals abroad, these schools also importantly serve French foreign policy objectives, promoting the French language itself as well as French culture and ideology, and thus form a valued component of France's cultural or "soft" diplomacy. The network of schools has been overseen since 1990 by the Agency for French Schools Abroad (Agence pour l'enseignement Français à l'étranger or AEFE) which is authorized by the French Ministry of Foreign Affairs (Ministère des Affaires étrangères) and is governed by directors who also represent the Ministry of National Education (Ministère de l'Éducation nationale) and includes several members of parliament as well (while the AEFE was only created in 1990, its predecessors in the Ministry of Foreign Affairs functioned with similar oversight).France is not unique in its more general policy of promoting a national language and culture as part of a larger foreign policy mission. The British Council has supported the study of English in over 100 countries since its founding in 1934. The Goethe Institute has had similar outreach for the German language and culture since 1951, and more recently the Confucius Institute, created in 2004, has multiple international partnerships to promote the study of Chinese. The United States government has also helped support some American schools overseas as well as English language educational opportunities through exchanges such as Fulbright programs. Institutions such as the American University of Cairo, the American University of Iraq at Sulaimani, and the American University of Beirut also help to promote American cultural values and traditions abroad, as Athanasios Moulakis, president of the American University of Iraq, has noted.[68]

However, France's dual mission of supporting French citizens abroad and of serving broader goals of French cultural diplomacy through supporting and promoting French schools abroad is unique. Promotion of the French language, culture and education has long been an integral part of both France's national educational policy and of France's foreign policy. An important aspect of this policy is the acknowledgement that French citizens have a right to French education. This policy, dating back to the Ferry laws, is often the subject of governmental studies, reports, and inquiries, and has sometimes resulted in surprisingly generous support for even wealthy elite French families abroad, as was the case when President Nicolas Sarkozy initiated a reform to "take charge" of tuition and fees for French private school students overseas in 2003.[69] The concern of the French government with the education of its citizens abroad can even be seen in studies such as those conducted by the French National Audit Court (Cour des comptes), which surveyed French citizens living abroad to determine the reason why their children do not attend French schools.

The wide appeal of these French schools abroad to citizens of other nations has helped to make them a valued arm of France's foreign policy, especially through what scholars of international relations and politics have called "soft power" or "cultural diplomacy." France today supports an international network of primary and secondary educational establishments, including the 492 French schools abroad in 137 countries, which serve over 350,000 students, of whom only approximately 40% are French citizens.[70] According to Olivier Boasson, the former Director of the Institut Français in Senegal, direct French government aid to these institutions today totals over €800 million.[71] The French government also devotes additional resources to the promotion of the French language abroad, including support for a network of over 1,000 chapters of the Alliance Française which offer French language courses and cultural activities in over 110 countries. Additionally, French embassies and consulates abroad offer financial and curricular support for the teaching of French as a foreign or second language in primary, secondary, and higher education institutions around the world through the Foreign Ministry's Cultural Affairs and

Education outreach offices. In the United States, for example, the French Embassy staff includes two full-time diplomats assigned to French education in North America and to the promotion of French schools in North America, in addition to several other education attachés assigned to specific geographic areas. More recently, the Institut Français, founded in 2010, was created "to act as the conduit for a new, more ambitious "diplomacy of influence", within the framework of French governmental policies and priorities."[72] The French Government has also invested directly in supporting French dual language and heritage language programs in public schools in the United States since approximately 2004.

As explained by Jean-Marie Guéhenno, a French diplomat and former Cultural Councilor at the French Embassy to the United States in New York, there are two motivating forces driving the development of France's extensive network of schools abroad:

> One is that for French citizens abroad, to have access to French schools is considered to be important. There is a demand by French people abroad that the French state makes sure that there are schools... I'd say that it's a French concern and that it's a concern for French citizens. The other is that throughout the world, [the network of schools] is an instrument of influence for France. [73]

As noted in the previous chapter, education and language are fundamental to French national identity. Through the period of nineteenth-century colonialism, especially with the vast expansion of France's presence abroad, this mission of ensuring French education to French citizens abroad played a large role in the establishment of these school networks. And although French children could continue to speak and learn French in other contexts, public education gave legitimacy that was essential to remaining French citizens. As explained by noted French historian and former *recteur d'université* Philippe Joutard, this link between language, education, and French national identity dates back to the Third Republic and is one of the most important justifications for the country's expansive network of schools abroad:

> France has long upheld a rather unique and systematic policy of international education for the very simple reason that

> since the beginning of the Third Republic in 1890, public
> education has been an important part of French republican
> identity... France is defined by its schools and its national
> education system, and so people realized that the best way to
> spread France's cultural influence throughout the world was
> not just through the Alliance Française, but through a
> network of schools. [74]

While institutions such as the Alliance Française are clearly designed
to appeal to students (of all ages) who wish to learn the French
language, a network of schools for children from nursery school
through high school must have a broader appeal.

Who Chooses to Study in French Schools Abroad?

The population of the French schools abroad is very diverse, but can
be broadly divided into three main groups: the children of French or
Francophone families living abroad, the children of local families,
and the children of a broader, international business and diplomatic
elite. Each group has its own reasons for attending a school in the
French network and each also helps to realize the mission, not only
of the individual school, but also of the French government.

According to Guéhenno, the French school network is especially
attractive to the world's highly mobile elites, such as diplomats and
business executives, who are drawn by the good reputation of the
French school system and the promise of mobility between French
schools around the world:

> [French] secondary schools still have a reasonably good
> reputation, so often you have part of the elite in the country
> that is interested in having their children go to French
> schools. Because there is that network, once you are hooked
> you have a whole class of people who can be moved around
> the world from Singapore to New York to London, and the
> fact that they will find a French Lycée in those places is
> important. [75]

Moreover, by attracting these elites and exposing them to French
language and culture, there is a hope that the network of schools will
build goodwill towards France among the world's elites. This helps

to explain why French education abroad is overwhelmingly focused on primary and secondary education, rather than the university level. As Guéhenno explains, "These are formative years. If the elite of a country has been trained in the French system, they will in some ways be better prepared to be supportive of and to be friendly with France."[76] Soft power theorist Joseph Nye would point out that cultural diplomacy is always a long game, and this is perhaps nowhere more apparent than in these schools. In other cases, the French school system can serve as an intellectual refuge in countries suffering under repressive regimes, as explained by Florent Verges, the Deputy Secretary General for External Affairs at the AEFE: in Spain and Portugal, for instance, many governmental officials are alumni of French schools, since under the dictatorships of Francisco Franco in Spain and António de Oliveira Salazar in Portugal, the French schools were some of the few places where it was possible to have a critical eye towards the regime, thereby attracting families involved in the opposition.[77]

Cultural Diplomacy and Soft Power Through Education

French politicians have always been aware of the role that France's language and culture play in maintaining its position on the stage of world politics, as demonstrated by the following comments by Xavier Darcos, the Minister of National Education under the government of French President Nicholas Sarkozy:

> There is more to the influence of a country than the strength of its economy, its strategic and military power and its place in the world institutions of governance. One must also consider how seductive are its ideas, its knowledge and its culture, and their relationship with the other factors of power.[78]

A few definitions help shape the manner in which this concept of "soft power" or "cultural diplomacy" applies to the subject of this study, French schools abroad. Efforts by one nation to extend its influence beyond its borders through expanding networks of artistic, cultural and educational activities represent a distinct form of "soft power" as opposed to such "hard power" efforts that include more direct economic or even military actions overseas, from trade agreements and military alliances to economic sanctions and war. Soft power efforts to expand the influence of one nation over others often have less direct or immediate impact, and they are often more loosely directed by a central government, yet they constitute a powerful means of achieving long –term foreign policy outcomes. As scholar of foreign policy and education Philip Coombs puts it, "nations have always engaged in activities that seek to project their policies and promote their power. The obvious instruments are war, diplomacy and economics, but culture has long been the 'fourth dimension' of international politics."[79]

France, perhaps more than any other nation, has made cultural diplomacy a hallmark of its foreign policies for centuries. France promoted its culture throughout Europe in the seventeenth and eighteenth centuries when the French language became the language of diplomacy and even the customary language used by some foreign courts, including in Prussia and in Russia. Through most of the nineteenth century, the values of the French Revolution—including the universal rights of Man, the rights of citizenship, and Republican values even under the Empire and the July Monarchy, and ironically perhaps through colonial conquests—were routinely exported via cultural and educational institutions through literature, art, and music, as well as actual schools. These efforts experienced stages, often corresponding to moments when France has had a particular need to assert or to defend its position on the global stage. One key moment marked the creation of the Alliance Française as a governmental institution to promote French language and culture abroad. American scholar of soft power, Joseph Nye observes that "after its defeat in the Franco-Prussian War, the French government sought to repair the nation's shattered prestige by promoting its language and literature through the Alliance Française created in 1883."[80]

There have been other key moments in history that have marked increased efforts in cultural diplomacy, both for France and for the United States. including the moment of the signing of the Treaty of Versailles which marked the first time such an international agreement would be signed not only in French, but also, at President Wilson's insistence, in English; a second moment was marked by France's reconstruction following World War II and more recently during the period after September 11, 2001 leading to the Iraq War, which France vigorously opposed in the United Nations.

While the promotion of French language and culture through institutions such as the Alliance Française was specifically aimed at non-French audiences, the promotion of French language and culture through networks of French schools abroad serves three distinct missions, reaching out not only to non-French audiences at both a local level (in the host country) but also at an international level (serving an elite corps of international diplomats and businessmen), while at the same time ensuring that French expatriates also have access to the critical components of national identity: language, literature, history, and geography.

According to political scientist Kevin Mulcahy, "French public diplomacy has been associated with its long-term view of itself as a depository of the world's cultural patrimony."[81] This idea of French "universalism" extends not only to the realms of "high culture" (arts and literature) but also to the French language itself.

The French tradition of cultural diplomacy extends back to the 16th century. Mulcahy cites Francois I's creation of the office of Superintendent des Batiments Royaux in 1535 as a landmark moment when French art treasures were to become the means of "projecting the image of France as the new Rome of cultural greatness."[82] The creation of a specific department within the Foreign Ministry to oversee cultural diplomacy after World War II further linked the promotion of the French language to the promotion of French culture and to French foreign policy more generally.

World War II left France diminished in international status: "Demoted after the war from the status of a minor major power to something decidedly less, France deployed its arts, and, especially, its language to gain a new place in the international system."[83] These efforts of cultural diplomacy were also especially important in the evolution of decolonization. Notably, Leopold Senghor, first President of the newly independent African country of Senegal, noted the importance of French and the newly coined term "Francophonie" to maintain the ongoing relationship between former colonies and France.[84]

French culture and language were also naturally linked to economic benefits and ultimately to international status:

> In brief, if the elites of the former colonies continued to write in French, they might more readily sign commercial contracts written in that language; and if cultures' elites everywhere continued to be open to the charms of French civilization including, variously, the export to the United States of French cooking (as both taught and mystified by Julia Child and associates), the books of French authors, and the traveling exhibitions of French artworks, then France could expect to bank a good deal of the international value of what Pierre Bourdieu calls "symbolic capital."[85]

Reassessing French cultural diplomacy after World War II meant that it was important both in France and in the United States for efforts of French cultural diplomacy to succeed in reestablishing not only the universality of French but also that status of France as a major power.

In terms of the position of the French language in the United States more generally, it was only after the National Defense of Education Act (1958) that foreign language studies in high schools and colleges began to rebound. Between 1958 and 1962, for example, the number of American high school students enrolled in French classes went from 479,769 in 1958 to 1,018,097 in 1962, an impressive increase of 112% in just four years—a much faster growth rate than Spanish and a much greater total number of students enrolled by 1962 than German.[86]

To a significant degree, France's culture can and has been identified with its schools. As Joutard explains, "the French have long realized that their culture isn't only transmitted through cultural events such as conferences and its theater [...] but also through the influence of France's schools," which are now present in most parts of the world.[87] In this sense, French schools do not only exist to educate the children of French speakers living abroad, but also to spread French language and French culture to the rest of the world: "French schools do not only exist to serve expatriates; the reason why the network is so vast is that these schools also exist for locals."[88] As Sean Lynch, who served as head of the Lycée Français de New York from 2011 to 2018 stated, "We do elect, with some constraints, to play that proactive role of cultural diplomacy... It's right at the heart of that sense of mission that we have."[89]

French Universalism

French schools have long made the claim that they are developing universal values, both in France and abroad:

> French schools are vehicles for French culture, which is founded on the French language but which also develops the idea of universality. I think that in France, like in the United States, we tend to think in universals... The French tend to think that what is good for the French is good for the rest of the world, and we tend to think in terms of humankind in general. There's a part of truth in this, since the philosophers of the eighteenth century dealt in universals, [a philosophy known as] humanism... Even today, the French tend to think in universals.[90]

There are essential contradictions in the mission of universalism, as can be seen, for example, in the controversy surrounding headscarves in French public schools; indeed, many French schools abroad have decided to adapt to, rather than resist local cultures, and in the French *lycées* of the Arab world, the wearing of headscarves is permitted even if it is forbidden for students attending public schools within the hexagon.

According to Philip Golub, a well-known professor of political science at the American University in Paris, French schools abroad are considered "almost as diplomatic institutions."[91] Golub tells an illuminating anecdote in which a student was slapped in the face by a French diplomat when he refused to stand for the American national anthem in protest of the Vietnam War:

> [He] actually walked down from the podium and slapped him
> in the face and explicitly told him that the French Lycée had
> diplomatic function and that France could not make political
> statements like that. There could be no public political
> statements at a French *lycée*. That shows how intimate the
> Quai d'Orsay is with the higher structures of the *lycées*.[92]

The incident was also covered in the *New York Times*.[93] Moreover, special events and award ceremonies at the Lycée were almost always attended by French dignitaries, including the Consul, the Ambassador to the United States, the Ambassador to the United Nations, and on some occasions the President of France, as with the inauguration of the school's new buildings by French President Chirac in 2003.

CHAPTER IV

The Huguenot, Refugees & French Education in New York Before 1934

The presence of French schools in the United States came much later than it did to many other parts of the world. Nonetheless, the importance of French as an international language, along with a growing interest in French language and French culture from the American Revolution to the present day, made the United States a hospitable environment for French education, especially beginning in the eighteenth and nineteenth centuries. However, the appearance of French schools in the United States and in New York followed a very different course than it did in French colonies or even in European capitals such as Berlin, Madrid, and Moscow, in large part because the United States was not a French colony. Indeed, whereas the first French schools abroad developed in tandem with other colonial institutions and were explicitly seen as an instrument to "civilize" the populations of the colonies, French schools in the United States always began as independent endeavors, supported by French speakers in the United States or American Francophiles. This chapter provides an overview of this historical context before delving into a case study of the Economical School of New York, an early example of a French school in the United States that illustrates some of the important trends that characterize the development of the French education in a non-colonial context.

Early History of French Education in the United States

Unlike the French schools developed by the Catholic missionaries in the French colonies, the French schools that developed in the United States were never explicitly intended to "convert" the local population. However, the continued existence and recent expansion of this network of schools, now directly governed by and at least in part financed by the French Ministry of National Education, continues to serve a dual role, both providing French education to Frenchmen abroad (a fundamental right of citizenship) and exercising a larger policy of public cultural diplomacy that continues to promote the French language and culture in an increasingly Anglicized world.

In the late eighteenth and early nineteenth century, the French language and culture generally enjoyed considerable prestige in the United States, initially coupled with the good will that resulted from the role of Lafayette's French forces in the American Revolution. However, this had not been the case through most of the seventeenth and early eighteenth century when France and the French Catholic church were generally vilified in the English colonies. For example, *The Convert*, a seventeenth-century American bestseller, tells the heroic tale of the conversion of a noble Huguenot Protestant away from the evils of the French Church.

According to some sources, the first formal teaching of French in what is now the United States began with French missionaries who taught French primarily to native tribes in the early seventeenth century.[94] Jesuit missionaries taught French to some of the native tribes they encountered, but there was little or no attempt to create formal schools. The revocation of the Edict of Nantes by Louis XIV in 1685 marked the end of an extended period of religious tolerance in France that resulted in a wave of Huguenot (French Protestant) emigrations, many along the same route that had taken English Puritans from Great Britain to the Netherlands and finally to American outposts in Massachusetts, New York and South Carolina.[95] However, these French-speaking immigrants did not necessarily seek an eventual return to France, nor did they attempt to ensure the continuous presence of French as a language of instruction—although the French language did continue to enjoy prestige and popularity in the United States.

Early eighteenth-century French settlements in New Rochelle, Charleston and in the cities of Mobile and New Orleans in Louisiana eventually grew to include small French schools which sometimes also attracted other local residents. There is also ample evidence of the popularity of French tutors in other major cities, including Boston and Philadelphia, where newspapers regularly advertised the services of French tutors, although there is little evidence of French being taught within schools or academies until the middle of the eighteenth century.

The years from 1750 to 1770 saw a general growth in the formal teaching of French in the American colonies, even though the use of French by settlers of French origin continued to decline in favor of English.[96] French instruction resumed at Harvard University, for example, after having been banned in 1735 following a disastrous earlier experience when Harvard's first French instructor experienced a religious conversion that threatened the sensitivities of the Harvard trustees.[97] After this incident, French was not allowed as an accredited course at Harvard until 1778, and a regularly appointed French instructor was not admitted to the faculty until 1797.[98]

In New York specifically, French settlers in New Amsterdam included the first doctor[99] and the first schoolmaster, who arrived in 1637, and by 1656 all government and town proclamations in New Amsterdam were issued in French as well as Dutch.[100] According to some accounts, in 1661 half of the inhabitants of Harlem were French Huguenots.[101]

Huguenot settlements in New York, dating to settlements of French Protestants from the early days of the New Amsterdam colony through British rule, continued to maintain a distinct French language and culture, including French-language schools, for example in New Paltz where the first schoolmaster Jean Cottin was given a house to live in 1689.[102] A significant French settlement also occurred at New Rochelle, such that one observer noted in his journal "many attend for the sole purpose of studying the idiom of a fashionable tongue" as well as in Manhattan where the French Church continued through the early nineteenth century to the present to offer Protestant services in the French language.[103]

These early French schools and churches served not only the local French Huguenot population, but also a number of English and Dutch settlers who were sent to the French grammar school in New Rochelle to acquire the language that had replaced Latin as the international language of diplomacy and commerce. Some knowledge of French was a valued sign, internationally and even in England, of prestige and social standing. However, it should be noted that these schools did not replace English as the language of instruction which was generally accepted in the United States, despite the fact that it was never designated an "official" language.[104] The development and popularity of French language learning was perhaps a testament to the success of efforts by France, dating back to the Ancien Régime, to ensure that French was to be the international language of diplomacy. The strong relationship between political activities and the promotion of French language and culture was well established by such powerful French officials as the Cardinals Richelieu and Mazarin who would "appoint literary academics as ambassadors in charge of the promotion of the French language."[105] Thus, it is not surprising that Americans who were to have significant diplomatic or government responsibilities would find French to be an important and useful tool. Among those reported to have studied at the French school in New Rochelle were John Jay, Washington Irving and General Philip Schuyler as well as the future American ambassador to France, Gouverneur Morris.[106] This period also saw a substantial increase in the publishing of French textbooks, and an increase in French books imported from abroad.

This exchange continued to grow during the period of the American Alliance with France through the American Revolution. However, American interest in the French language and French culture generally experienced a sharp decline in reaction to the excesses of the French Revolution, and declined further during the hostility generated by the XYZ Affair in 1798[107]. Although there continued to be a generally favorable attitude towards the language, the eminent physician, statesman and educator, Benjamin Rush expressed some of this reaction in his article "Thoughts upon Female Education" written for *Columbia Magazine* in 1798:

> I beg leave further to bear testimony against the practice of making the French language a part of female education in America. In Britain where company and pleasure are the principal business of ladies where the nursery and the kitchen form no part of their care, and where a daily intercourse is

maintained with French-men and other foreigners who speak the French language, knowledge of it is necessary. But the case is widely different in this country... Let it not be said in defense of knowledge of the French language that many elegant books are written in it. Those of them that are truly valuable are translated; but if this were not the case, the English language certainly contains many more books of real utility and useful information that can be read without neglecting other duties, by the daughter, or wife of an American citizen.[108]

Rush also objected to instructing American women in music and drawing, activities which he felt would detract from time better spent on philosophy, literature and perfecting the English language.

This reaction against French language and culture was relatively short-lived, and a new wave of Francophone immigration, this time primarily from the West Indies following the Revolution in Santo Domingo (Haiti), created a renewed interest in French education, particularly in New York and Louisiana, areas where some of the estimated 30,000 mostly well-educated middle- and upper-class refugees settled. Of particular interest during this period is the Economical School, a school created in New York City in 1810 for the benefit of "poor refugees from Santo Domingo" which serves as a window into several ongoing developments in public education, both in the United States and in France at the time. Established just two years after the creation of the French National Ministry of Education, and directed by several prominent Frenchmen as well as by Americans active in local government and in New York's own fledgling public-school movement, the school's fifteen-year history offers evidence of an early official collaboration among international educators. This school also marks the first time that the purpose of French instruction appears to have extended beyond the simple acquisition of French as a foreign language. Much like the French schools abroad that were created in the twentieth century, the Economical School was intended to help French citizens eventually return to France, while also serving some local families in New York who did not return.

The Baron Hyde de Neuville and
the Foundation of the Economical School

The founder of the Economical School in New York was a wealthy French royalist, Baron Guillaume Hyde de Neuville. Hyde de Neuville had been living in exile during most of the years following the French Revolution and took refuge in New York after the failure of his negotiations with Napoleon on behalf of the Bourbon monarchs. From the launching of the school in New York, Hyde de Neuville clearly saw the dual roles of the school that would emerge in future French schools in New York as well. There was always an intent to serve local students who wished to learn French as well as exiles who hoped to return to France. Hyde de Neuville's wife, a prolific amateur artist, documented much of their stay in America with watercolors and drawings, including many rare views of Indian tribes and early settlements in upstate New York, as well as, remarkably, the students at the Economical School where she herself also instructed.[109] Concerned with the plight of refugees fleeing the former French colony of Saint-Domingue after the Haitian Revolution, Hyde de Neuville decided to take matters into his own hands and found a school where the children of these refugees could continue to receive a French education.

Hyde de Neuville's decision to found a school reflects a remarkable confluence of events and interest. French immigration to New York in the years following 1792 were mostly middle class or members of the aristocracy, and many of their children had already been attending French schools or benefited from tutoring in France or Santo Domingo before their arrival in New York. Many also returned to France after the fall of Napoleon in 1815, and some would even return to the United States as successful businessmen or, as in the case of Hyde de Neuville, as representatives of the newly restored Bourbon monarchy in France (Hyde de Neuville also served as the French ambassador to Washington from 1816 to 1821). Not all were well-to-do, however, and some arrived from Santo Domingo following the Haitian revolution nearly destitute, although the new Haitian government's decision to pay $60 million in reparations for French property on the island over the following 60 years did result in substantial income for some of the families living in New York

(Haiti paid at a rate of $1 million per year until the island was essentially bankrupt in 1850, with payments exceeding an astonishing $450 million in current US dollars). Therefore, the school was designed to be "economical," that is to say affordable to all, with only a minimal tuition and a strong focus on providing a decent education to New York City's poor, especially those speaking French.

The Economical School in the City of New York was incorporated by an act of the New York State legislature on March 10th, 1810. According to Article I of its *Regulations*, the school was established "to promote instruction, to render it economical, and to afford some education to the children of French immigrants and other strangers."[110]

The school was originally located on Chapel Street (now West Broadway), between Duane and Reed, before being moved to Anthony Street (now Worth Street), opposite the New York Hospital.[111] According to contemporary accounts, in its new location the school was housed in a substantial building: "the building was large, has [sic.] two wings and a steeple, with a bell in it stood on open ground."[112] The printing press for the school, which eventually printed French and other foreign language materials as well, was located nearby at 59 Church Street and was operated by the school's students.[113]

According to the *Regulations* cited above, the school was organized into two classes, a lower class of students aged twelve or younger who would be taught reading and writing in French and in English as well as arithmetic, organized "upon the plan of Lancaster." The second class was composed of older students or any who could "read and write well enough to perform the exercises of the class. This second class was "confined to the study of the French language, the general principles of grammar, geography, history and mathematics" and eventually mechanical drawing and bookkeeping. Additional "persons as may wish to attend, for the purpose of learning French" were also admitted, but strict rules about tuition and attendance were enforced even for these students. Tuition was on a sliding scale "from two shillings to three dollars per quarter, according to the rate determined by the inspectors." Books and materials, as well as firewood, were also to be paid for by the scholars, except in cases of financial hardship.[114]

The Trustees of the Economical School

The *Regulations* also state that the school was governed by a board of nine trustees. The founding members of the board are listed as follows: Benjamin Moore, Victor Moreau, Hyde de Neuville, Charles Wilkes, John B. Lombart, William MacNeven, John R. Murray, Thomas Eddy, and Clement C. Moore.[115] Benjamin Moore was the school's first President, Victor Moreau the first Vice President, Hyde de Neuville the first Secretary, and Charles Wilkes the first Treasurer.[116] These trustees were responsible for the hiring of teachers and were involved in the day-to-day running of the school. Indeed, it is known that the Baron and Baroness Hyde de Neuville frequently visited the school and grew very close to their students, as is testified by the Baroness's series of watercolors in the Economical School series, which depict students involved in a variety of school-related activities.[117] Some trustees also taught classes at the school, including Victor Moreau and John Lombart. According to Barrett, both Hyde de Neuville and Victor Moreau would visit the school daily: "every morning, Hyde de Neuville and General Moreau would go to the school, and give lectures and explanations to the scholars."[118] The continued involvement of the school's founder and trustees highlights the philanthropic nature of the endeavor, as well as the importance of the school's mission.

The list of the Economical School's trustees includes several names that deserve further attention, including trustees who were active in state and local government as well as several notable French expatriates and officials. Indeed, Hyde de Neuville's philanthropic venture required considerable financial and political support, and its initial success would not have been possible without the early involvement of a number of influential New Yorkers, several of whom served on the board of trustees. Benjamin Moore, for instance, was the President of Columbia University, then known as Columbia College; his son, Clement C. Moore, was a poet. Charles Wilkes was a wealthy and well-known financier as well as the President of the Bank of New York. William MacNeven was an Irish physician in exile who taught chemistry and obstetrics at the New York College of Physicians and Surgeons. Thomas Eddy was a Quaker philanthropist and politician who had served as the governor of the New York Hospital and had been involved in prison reform in New York State, and who like Wilkes was a member of the New York Free School Society. These connections guaranteed Hyde de Neuville the financial and the political support he needed to start the school; it was Thomas Eddy who petitioned the New York State legislature to incorporate the school in 1810.[119]

However, the list of prominent New Yorkers associated with the Economical School goes beyond the original nine trustees, and the Economical School operated in close cooperation with the New York City government, and the *Regulations* stipulate that "the Mayor, recorder, aldermen and assistants of the City of New York shall and may be ex-officio members of [the Economical School society]." The school also received early support from Henry Cruger, a wealthy New York businessman whose father had been the mayor, as well as DeWitt Clinton, who was then the President of the Free School Society.[120] A rising star and influential figure in New York State politics, Clinton played a central role in the history of the Economical School, bringing material as well as political support to the school's development. In a letter dated April 11, 1809, Hyde de Neuville petitions Clinton, who was then serving as the Mayor of New York and the President of the New York State Senate, for his support, citing Clinton's involvement in education reform:

> I have the honor of addressing you on the plan of a liberal institution. You are so well known to be a zealous protector of all establishments of this kind, that I believe myself sufficiently authorized in claiming in favor of this one, your benevolent interest.
>
> Deign, Sir, to place your name first on the list of actual members of the society—it will assure the success of this institution.[121]

Hyde de Neuville's request did not go unanswered, and on March 6, Clinton made the following report to the New York State legislature:

That the said institution was originally founded for the education of poor persons driven by the unfortunate events of war in foreign parts; that it has since been extended to the indigent of all nationalities; that it is formed on the celebrated plan of Lancaster; contains upward of 200 scholars; is calculated to be eminently useful, and is supported principally by the founders. It is, therefore, the opinion of the committee that it is justly entitled to the favorable notice of the State.[122]

A bill was then read on the Senate floor, and the society of the Economical School in New York was incorporated the next day. Clinton was also instrumental in the passage of a law empowering the Mayor to levy a tax on the citizens of New York and to distribute the funds to the trustees of the Free School Society, including the trustees of the Economical School. [123] Clinton continued to be involved with the Economical School throughout its history, later serving as the President of the society.

A good number of the school's early supporters were prominent French emigrants, illustrating the school's strong connection to France and to the French language, despite Hyde de Neuville's opposition to the current regime. Victor Moreau, for instance, was a French general who had helped elevate Napoleon Bonaparte to power, but who was banished to the United States following his involvement in a plot to assassinate the Emperor. The original list of trustees also shows that Hyde de Neuville managed to secure the support of John B. Lombart, the Chancellor of the French Consulate and therefore the official representative of the French government in New York; this is surprising considering Hyde de Neuville's strong royalist ties, but suggests that Hyde de Neuville and Lombart were able to put aside their political differences in order to provide an affordable education for French speakers in New York.[124] Indeed, in his memoirs Hyde de Neuville describes his petition to the French government in order to secure support for French refugees fleeing the colonies:

Let us recall that the Economical School, which I founded during my exile in the United States, was created for the poor children of Saint-Domingue. I had brought this tragedy to the Minister's attention.

I asked for the government to occasionally send a frigate to help transport those poor French citizens who could not return to France, unable to afford the cost of the journey.[125]

Moreover, the French Chancellor Lombart's involvement with the school was more than just a formality. According to Hyde de Neuville's biographer, Lombart was one of the main professors at the school, teaching French, history, geography, and English.[126] The fact that an official representative of the French government was so involved in the day-to-day running of the school highlights the close connection to France the Economical School maintained throughout its history, and suggests that a French curriculum and pedagogical methods were adopted from the outset.

Finally, the Economical School also received early support from Cheverus, the French Bishop of Boston, and the list of trustees published in the second issue of the *Journal des Dames* includes Father Vianney, a French Carmelite preacher who worked extensively with refugees from Santo Domingo, as well as Labiche de Reignefort, himself a refugee from the French colony.[127] Later trustees of the Economical School included the French emigrant doctors Cognacq and Evrard.[128]

There is reason to believe that the combination of French and American trustees on the board of the Economical School was fairly remarkable for its time. In an address delivered to the Free School Society, DeWitt Clinton notes that the school "is cherished by French and American gentlemen, of great worth and respectability, who are entitled to every praise for their benevolence."[129] The fact that the trustees of the school included both New York politicians and French diplomats such as the Consul Lombart points to a remarkable confluence of French and American interests, at least in regard to the influx of French-speaking refugees from the former colonies. This is particularly significant given the fact that diplomatic relations between France and the United States at the time were lukewarm at best, the United States remaining neutral in the Napoleonic Wars and restrictions on trade between the two countries still in place despite the repealing of the Embargo Act in 1809, just one year before the founding of the school.[130]

Curriculum and Language of Instruction

There is an ambiguity concerning the primary language of instruction at the Economical School. According to the articles of incorporation adopted by the New York State assembly, the Economical School was established "for the education of the children of French emigrants, resident in the city of New York, in the English language and literature."[131] The school's own regulations, on the other hand, do not indicate that English was the only or even the primary medium of instruction. Article I, for instance, agrees with the articles of incorporation that the school was established to "afford some education to the children of French immigrants and other strangers."[132]

On the other hand, Article VI suggests that this education was in fact carried out in two languages: "In the lowest class shall be taught reading, and writing, in English & French and arithmetic."[133] Article VIII places even more importance of French language instruction with the provision that "the second class shall be chiefly confined to the study of the French language," and Article XX outlines the school's plan for French language classes for non-students over the age of fifteen, who were granted a special status:

> In the school room there shall be a form for such persons as may wish to attend, for the purpose of learning French, without being subjected to the rules imposed upon the regular scholars. No scholar of this description shall be admitted under the age of fifteen years, and the terms of admission shall be three dollars per quarter, payable in advance.[134]

All this seems to suggest that French was the predominant language at the school, although instruction was almost certainly carried out in both English and in French. One of the Baroness de Neuville's watercolors, for instance, depicts a student translating a text with the title "l'école française" in French and "the French school" in English, suggesting a bilingual pedagogy.[135] Several issues of the *Journal des Dames*, a monthly magazine printed by the school's press, contain bilingual texts that were in all likelihood used as pedagogical aids.

Unlike many of the previous French establishments in the United States (in New Paltz or New Rochelle, for example), the Economical School clearly maintained links to France throughout its history. The prominence of French in the Economical School's curriculum is just one aspect of the school's commitment to educating children in the French language and French culture. Guided by Hyde de Neuville's commitment to classical education, the school remained close to French literary tastes and scholarship: for example, the edition of the *Fables de la Fontaine* published by the Economical School press was accompanied by a commentary by Jean-François de La Harpe, a French writer and literary critic, and one issue of the Journal on modern literature simply reproduced a lecture given by La Harpe and the Lycée de Paris.[136] Moreover, the Economical School's edition of the *Fables* is accompanied by many explicatory footnotes, many of which provide definitions or notes on grammatical usage, as well as clarifying La Fontaine's historical or mythological references.

The students' textbooks included parts of the new national curriculum and the school followed practices (awarding honors, for example) that were integral to public education in France. For instance, Barrett explains that "the school had grand examinations every year" in the tradition of French public education. Barrett also cites this inscription on the back of a student's copy of the *Fables de la Fontaine*, written in Hyde de Neuville's hand:

> Prix de bonne conduite accordé à Miss Hostin le 9 juillet 1810, par les membres du comité inspecteur de l'école.
> (Signed) G. HYDE NEUVILLE
> (Signed) LOMBART. Instituteur.[137]

The Economical School's French-inspired curriculum ensured that some of its best students could return to France to complete their studies. The most notable of these is perhaps Phillippe Ricord. The son of a royalist family that had fled to the United States after the French Revolution, Ricord was one of the Economical School's first students, being included on the register in 1810.[138] Ricord completed his primary education at the school, after which he turned to odd jobs to support himself in the United States. He also had the opportunity to participate in several research expeditions with his brother, a natural scientist, and it was during this time that he first met Charles

Alexandre Lesueur, the French naturalist and explorer. When Hyde de Neuville returned to the United States in 1816 as the Ambassador of France, he found his former student and took advantage of his position to facilitate Ricord's return to France. In 1820, Hyde de Neuville ordered Ricord to collect and deliver zoological specimens to the Museum of Natural History in Paris, with the agreement of Lesueur.[139] He sent his former student off with a letter of introduction to Georges Cuvier, the eminent French naturalist and professor of natural history at the Collège de France.[140] Thanks to Hyde de Neuville's recommendation, the brothers were appointed as curators of the collection; to supplement his modest income, Ricord taught English lessons and translated some works of natural history.[141] Ricord was soon admitted to the Faculty of Medicine at the Academy of Val-de-Grâce, and he eventually became a well-known physician and a specialist of venereal disease. Ricord was forever grateful to his former teacher Hyde de Neuville for the instruction he had received at the Economical School. The following passage is taken from Ricord's biography in the bulletins of the Paris surgical society:

> Ricord never forgot the important service that had been done to him by his eminent protector. Many years later, once he had achieved recognition in Paris, he was visited in his private hotel on the rue de Tournon by the Baron Hyde de Neuville, who exclaimed: "What magnificence! My friend, I could get lost in your palace." "How is that possible," responded Ricord, "since it's you who built it." [142]

However, despite stories like Ricord's and the Economical School's dependence on the French curriculum and teaching methods, it seems as if most of the school's students easily integrated into American life. As Barrett puts it, "American they were, although of French parentage, and some of the first merchants [of New York] now bear their names."[143] Hyde de Neuville's biographer also finds that most of these students never returned to France, instead marrying Americans and settling in the United States.[144] Both she and Barrett cite the story of Jane Hostin, the daughter of James Hostin, a refugee from Saint-Domingue who became a wine merchant in New York. His tavern, writes Barrett, was a meeting-point for French emigrants who had stayed in America, whether out of choice or misfortune: "It was a place of resort for old Frenchmen. Mr. Hostin was one of those unfortunate persons driven out of St. Domingo... He lost his all, and like many others, who escaped from that Island, had to commence the world anew in New York."[145] Like many others, Jane and James Barrett never returned to France, although the daughter's time at the Economical School shows that they remained close to their language and their culture.

Furthermore, in the unique circumstances of early nineteenth century New York, the school benefited from the enthusiasm of American educators for the recently developed Lancastrian system of monitorial education, and thus became an early example of the international spread of Joseph Lancaster's ideas on education for the masses (his 1803 book, *Improvements in Education*, was translated into French in 1813). Indeed, Article VI of the *Regulations of the Economical School* explicitly states that instruction "shall be conducted upon the plan of Lancaster."

In addition, the bylaws of the school, adopted by the trustees in April 1810, include some notable educational innovations. An early example of current-day non-discriminatory policies, Article I of the *Regulations* states:

> The objects of the Society are, to promote instruction, to render it economical, and to afford some education to the children of French emigrants and other strangers. The School shall be open to children of either sex, without distinction of nation, religion or fortune.

Like many other charity schools at the time, the Economical School was committed to moral and religious instruction, with the hopes that this type of education would eventually eradicate poverty. At the same time, Article V insists on religious neutrality, perhaps reflecting the ongoing debates in France about religious education, which would not be resolved until the Ferry Laws of 1883 created a system of public secular schools:

> The object of the institution, being to propagate morality and religion in general, without interfering with the particular tenets in which parents may desire to educate their children, no book shall be made use of, for the instruction of the

scholar, unless it shall have been previously submitted to the perusal of two persons, named for that purpose, by the Trustees, one of whom shall be a catholic, and the other a protestant.

The school thus appears to have been truly progressive for its day and was more concerned with the general moral education of the poor than their conversion to one or another particular denomination. This was a distinction that made the Economical School unique among the private schools that were present in New York at the time. Some, such as the Trinity School created in 1809, for example, and which has continued to flourish, were created through the Anglican Church's Society for the Propagation of the Gospel in Foreign Parts, which sponsored charity schools throughout the British Empire.

School Finances

The school supported itself through modest tuition—hence the name "economical school" meant to designate the fact that it would be affordable to all—as well as through some City and State government funds allocated to the institution. A report by the Comptroller's office of the State of New York assessed that the school was paid $1000 in 1810 and $500 every year thereafter until 1825, when the school ceased to operate.[146] Given that tuition was on a sliding scale between two shilling and three dollars a quarter, this amounted to a significant annual contribution, equivalent to the yearly tuition of approximately fifty scholars.

The Economical School was also in large part funded by charitable donations. Gloria Deák reports that the original school building was financed with a combination of City funds and private donations: "petitioning the city's Common Council for a building, they matched their request with their own successful fundraising."[147] This is confirmed by the *Regulations of the Economical School*, which indicate that the trustees were soliciting donations to finance the construction of a new school building. In addition to the financial support provided by the many wealthy patrons and trustees of the Economical School, a number of public charity events were organized to help secure the funds necessary to start the school. In his memoirs, Hyde de Neuville writes that there were balls and concerts organized to raise money for the school, and that they were widely attended by New York's high society. [148] Those whose contributions attained a certain level were admitted as members of the Economical School society. To that effect, the *Regulations of the Economical School* include the following provision:

> Any person who shall subscribe and contribute ten dollars to the benefit of said society shall by virtue of such contribution be a member of the said corporation. In addition, those who contributed fifty dollars to the Economical School earned the right during their lifetime to send one child to the school free of charge.[149]

Finally, the Economical School was also able to support itself through its press. Between January and December of 1810, the school published a monthly journal called the *Journal des Dames*, which was meant to raise money in addition to providing an outlet for the students and the school's founder. An editor's note at the end of the first issue of the journal indicates that "subscriptions are solicited for the support of this useful institution [the Economical School]" and that "the annual subscription is 4 dollars." The journal had a fairly wide distribution, with the editors of the journal receiving correspondence from New York, Baltimore, Boston, Philadelphia, and Charleston. As Watel puts it, the *Journal*, and more generally speaking the press of the Economical School, was by and for the students of the school.[150]

The objectives of the *Journal* were not purely philanthropic or cultural. In all probability was also meant as a pedagogical aid for the students of the Economical School, as is made clear in the editor's note appearing at the beginning of each issue of the *Journal*: "our journal primarily aims to shape the taste of young people."[151]

The *Journal* also illustrates the relationship of De Neuville and the Economical School to French and English. Although the *Journal* wasn't an entirely bilingual publication, some sections were written in English. One story was even published in a side-by-side translation, titled "Cela sera, cela doit être" in French and "It Shall, It Must Be So" in English.[152] According to Watel, this is most likely because the story was designed to be read and studied in class at the

Economical School, which had French as well as American students and which was itself a bilingual institution.[153] Particularly interesting in this regard is the presence of a footnote defining the word "onc" in the text, which Watel interprets as a sure sign of the story's pedagogical value since its presence would only make sense in a text meant to be read by children.[154] The readership was most likely similarly bilingual, as testified by English-language classifieds and letters from readers eager to learn the French language.

Perspectives on the Economical School

According to contemporary accounts, the Economical School was an academic success. Barrett writes that "the best professors in the Union were employed" by the school and refers to "the celebrated economical school"[155] in his brief description of the school's history. Even more remarkable is a "highly laudatory report of the method of teaching at the French school" that was delivered by a special committee appointed by the Common Council of the City of New York.[156] With its decision to incorporate the school in 1810, the Common Council gave the school two lots and a substantial financial contribution, and made the following report on the school:

> Having attended to the mode of instruction in said school, and having witnessed the improvement of the pupils, they are of opinion, that the institution is admirably calculated to be of extensive utility; and from the circumstance of teaching a foreign as well as the language of this country must be beneficial not only to emigrants [sic.] children; but also to those of our own citizens. The respectable character of the Trustees and the indefatigable philanthropy of Monsieur Neufville [sic.] its principal conductor excites a confidence, that any grant made by this Board will be properly applied and extensively promote the wishes and views of the friends of literature.[157]

Thus, the Council gave its endorsement, not only of the school, but also of the principle that teaching another language in addition to English would be generally beneficial for students in New York. Two centuries later, similar ideas would be at the core of the creation of new French programs for Francophone immigrants as we will see in ensuing chapters.

The Economical School and the Origins of Public Education in New York City

As a member of the Free School Society of New York City, the Economical School played a part in the early history of public education in New York City, in particular through its mission to provide an "economical" education in a nondenominational setting. According to its articles of incorporation, the purpose of the Free School Society, of which De Witt Clinton was the founding President and to which the Economical School belonged since its inception in 1810, was "to extend the means of education to such poor children as do not belong to, or are not provided for, by any religious society." [158] As explained by William Oland Bourne, the first historian of the New York Public School Society, the Free School Society was the first organization of its kind in the City of New York to bear the responsibility of "providing a *common school education* for the masses of people."[159] The Free School Society and the schools that belonged to it thus represent an early attempt to provide a public and secular education to the children of New York City, a project which is roughly contemporaneous with the similar developments taking place in the French education system thanks to the laws passed by the French Minister of Public Instruction François Guizot.[160]

Public education was far more developed in France, especially under Napoleon, than it was in the United States as a whole, which had under the Constitution relegated matters concerning education to the states and not the federal government. In New York State, it is significant that the Economical School, a French institution, was involved in the birth of public education in New York; the nondenominational focus of the Economical School and of the Free School Society echoes the important role played by secularism (*laïcité*) in the development of the French public school system, although the schools of the Free School Society were by no means secular institutions and the mission of the Society was explicitly conceived as a moral one: "It will be a primary object, without observing the particular forms of any religious society, to inculcate the sublime truths of religion and morality contained in the Holy

Scriptures."[161] Nevertheless, the fact that these schools were not tied to any particular religious institution or denomination is significant and was the first step in building a system of public education in New York City.

The Economical School also played a role in the development of public education in New York through its implementation of the Lancastrian system of education. As discussed above, the Lancaster method was written into the *Regulations of the Economical School*, and the system was in many ways the centerpiece of the school's educational philosophy. The Lancaster system, which was popularized in 1803 when the London schoolmaster Joseph Lancaster published his influential pamphlet, *Improvements in Education*, was based on the monitorial system, an education system developed by Quakers Robert Raikes and Andrew Bell in the late eighteenth century whereby the older or the stronger students taught the younger or weaker pupils. The method was perhaps an early example of an attempt at globalization in education, as it generated non-denominational schools through Lancastrian societies both in Great Britain and in France.

According to John F. Reigart, a historian of the Lancasterian system of education in the schools of New York City, the Lancaster plan was "the most popular means of elementary education during the first half of the nineteenth century."[162] Indeed, the Lancasterian system became the basis for education in England, and it was adopted as the national system of Ireland, as well as in Scotland and the British colonies of India, Canada, South Africa, and the West Indies[163]. Although the implementation of the Lancasterian system across the Anglophone world was never a centralized or standardized process, it does in some ways resemble the spread of French schools throughout the world during the nineteenth century, particularly through the efforts of the French Lay Mission (Mission laïque française or MLF) in the French colonies. The trustees of the Free School Society of New York City frequently turned to the more-established Lancasterian schools in England for guidance in their efforts to develop the Lancasterian system in the United States. For instance, "in 1818, they imported a teacher, Charles Picton, from the parent school in London; in 1820, they issued a manual based on that of the British and Foreign School Society for 1816; and in 1818, they welcomed the author of the system, Joseph Lancaster." [164] The parallels with the MLF are striking, particularly the practice of assigning teachers and importing curricular materials from abroad, although once again it is important to stress that the dissemination of the Lancasterian system throughout the world was nowhere near as systematic as the efforts of the MLF.

One of the major advantages of the Lancaster system was its affordability. By assigning teaching and disciplinary duties to students, schools were not required to pay as many adults to fulfill those responsibilities, and the methods of instruction, such as the use of slates instead of pen and paper as well the use of reading-sheets instead of books, were similarly conceived as a means to reduce the cost of education: "The same desire to economize, which was the first motive for the use of monitors, was also the first motive for changes in methods of instruction."[165] As such, the Lancaster system was an obvious choice for the Economical School and more generally speaking all of the schools of the Free School Society. Indeed, John Reigart sees the introduction of the Lancasterian system as an important step in the direction of public education in New York City, if only by the fact that they drastically increased the number of children who had access to an affordable education: "To supply education to the thousands of neglected children there was at hand a ready-made plan, remarkably cheap in operation, and, with all its faults, apparently superior in method and discipline to the schools of the day."[166] Through its implementation of the Lancasterian system, the Economical School was participating in a much larger movement of educational reform with the express purpose of increasing access to education among the city's poor. By 1825, the Economical School Society had been dissolved and incorporated into the Public School Society, thereby guaranteeing the school's place in the history of public education in New York City: "For the Economical School Society this union with the latter was a perfectly natural result, with Clinton as its president and with aims identical to those of the Free School Society."[167]

Finally, the role that Dewitt Clinton, the Governor of New York, played in the success of the Economical School, particularly in relation to the early history of public education in New York City, is highly significant. Clinton's political activism, along with his educational views, played an important part in shaping the Economical School's educational philosophy and set the course for the development of a public-school system in New York City. Clinton's view of education was fundamentally democratic: as Edward Fitzpatrick explains in his historical study of Clinton's educational views, Clinton saw education as "the absolutely indispensable foundation to democracy."[168] There are numerous examples defending this thesis in Clinton's writings and addressed to the State legislature, such as the following message to the State legislature from 1825: "Upon education we must therefore rely for the purity, the preservation and the perpetuation of the republican government."[169] Fitzpatrick goes on to explain that the introduction of the Lancasterian system played an important part in the realization of this vision, as did the project to extend the benefits of education to the most disadvantaged segments of New York's population, including the Economical School's mission to educate refugees from Saint Domingue.[170]

In conclusion, although the Economical School was founded by a French royalist, taught classes in French, and primarily catered to a French-speaking population, the school played an important part in the early history of education in New York City. Through its mission to educate the children of refugees at an affordable cost and without excluding children based on their religious denomination, as well as through its implementation of the Lancasterian system and the support offered by Dewitt Clinton, the Economical School is an excellent case study of the institutions from which developed a system of public instruction in New York City.

French Education in New York from 1825 to 1934

After the closing of the Economical School in 1825, several other French schools appeared in New York, including Mademoiselle Charbonnier's French Protestant Boarding and Day School on East 36th Street and Mademoiselle Rostan's French, English, and German Boarding and Day School on East 41st Street.[171] These schools appear to have been primarily for learning and practicing the French language and there does not seem to have been any direct connection to the French national curriculum or to the French government itself. Similarly, the Institute Tisné School for Girls on Riverside Drive in Manhattan, which operated from 1894 to 1933, served a small number of upper middle-class families who valued the prestige of a French education. Instruction was carried out in French as well as English, as testified by the school's two-sided report cards, with one page for grades in French subjects and the other for English.[172] However, unlike the schools run by Mademoiselle Charbonnier and Mademoiselle Rostan, the Institut Tisné was endorsed by the French Minister of Public Instruction as well as the Alliance Française, informally anticipating the process of accreditation that characterizes the network of French schools abroad today.[173] Henryette Tisné, the headmistress and founder of the school, was an active member of the Alliance Française, and served as a delegate for New York City at the annual meeting of the general assembly of the Federation of the Alliance Française of the United States and Canada in April 1923.[174] Following the death of Madame Tisné, the institute continued only briefly under the direction of her son Walter, closing definitively in 1933. Finally, there were also a number of kindergartens that had been opened by French teachers, including one on 95th Street near where the Lycée itself would eventually be located. However, by 1934 there was no French school available in New York City where the children of French diplomats and other French expatriates and American Francophiles could send their children.

CHAPTER V

French Education in New York After 1934 & The Lycée Français de New York

By the 1930s, there were a number of French schools internationally that delivered the French curriculum and were considered "French Lycées." These included schools with fully French curricula attached in some way to the French national education system, usually with some oversight from the overseas services of the Ministry of Foreign Affairs, including schools in Berlin, Madrid, and London, in addition to the network of colonial schools run by the church and the French Lay Mission. These schools often served some local elites, but primarily existed for the benefit of the children of French diplomats and other French families. However, no such school existed in New York or even in the United States at that time, even though the French population of New York State was estimated to be over 32,000.[175] It was in this context that Charles Ferry de Fontnouvelle, the Consul General of France in New York, raised the idea of starting such a school with the French Ambassador to the United States and a number of prominent Americans. This idea would eventually lead to the founding of the Lycée Français de New York (LFNY) in 1935, the school where I would have a long teaching career from 1973 to 2003.

The Creation of the Lycée Français de New York and Its Early Years

According to Alain Dubosclard, a historian of French cultural diplomacy in the twentieth century, the idea to create the LFNY first appears in a letter from Charles de Fontnouvelle to the *Service des oeuvres françaises à l'étranger*, an agency of the French Ministry of Foreign Affairs responsible for France's cultural actions abroad.[176] In his letter, the Consul advanced three main arguments for the creation of a *lycée* in New York. First, de Fontnouvelle cited the precedent of the *lycées* in London, Madrid, and Berlin, other major international cities with a significant French presence. Secondly, he pointed to the demographic shifts taking place within the population of French expatriates in the United States: generally speaking, their social status was increasing, which meant that a larger number of French children were seeking to prolong their education through secondary school; however, due to the lack of a French *lycée*, they were forced to integrate the American school system, which de Fontnouvelle believed would cause them to permanently lose their ties to France. Thirdly, he cited the growing interest in the French language and French culture among Americans, and argued that the new *lycée* would be able to take in several American students in the hope that they would develop an affinity towards France through their schooling in the French system.[177]

The circumstances for the founding of the LFNY were both propitious and somewhat inauspicious. On the positive side, French language, culture and education enjoyed considerable prestige in the United States, having largely replaced German as the predominant foreign language to be studied in the wake of World War I. Moreover, as Whitney Walton observed in her book about internationalism, national identities, and study abroad programs in France and the United States, by the end of World War I France had by and large replaced Germany as the most desirable destination for advanced studies by American students. In France there was concern by the French Foreign Ministry about the decline of French in the United States—both in daily usage and in foreign language studies. In the United States and especially in New York, French language and culture continued to enjoy prestige even while Franco-Americans in Louisiana and New England struggled to maintain their language. In line with the growing prestige of the French education system in academic circles, leading educators including President Griswold of Yale routinely awarded two years' academic credit to students from France who had completed the rigorous French baccalaureate examinations at the end of their *lycée* or high school years, so that they entered college as juniors.[178]

On the other hand, in the 1930s there was also widespread distrust of foreign institutions, and in New York efforts by both Germany and Italy to establish schools were met with considerable resistance. The

French were acutely aware of the risk that cultural diplomacy might be viewed negatively as propaganda. Furthermore, even among pro-French Americans, the fear of a leftist "Front Populaire" government in France raised concerns that socialist or communists might gain control of an official French establishment in New York.

The creation of a French school that was incorporated as an American private institution distinguished the LFNY from other French *lycées* abroad. According to Pierre Brodin, the Lycée's first Director of Studies, "it was decided from the outset that the future lycée would be an *American* institution, registered and administered according to American laws by a Board of Trustees with a majority of American members."[179] Similarly, Dubsoclard explains that de Fontnouvelle knew full well that the *lycée* in New York could only exist as an American private school, free from both French interference and from direct supervision by New York State, although the school would have to obey American laws and follow American educational standards as well as the official French curriculum. This status would grant the school a certain degree of independence from the French government, and therefore the autonomy to implement its own curriculum, making adaptations if necessary to the highly detailed instructions sent regularly by the Ministry of National Education through its *Bulletin officiel*; finally, as a private school, the Lycée would be able to seek donations from private individuals, something that even today is largely seen in a negative light in France.[180]

Supporters of the Lycée were always careful to distance themselves from the idea that the school was an arm of the French government, or an instrument to promote France's interests in the United States. For instance, Dr. Stephen Duggan, the director of the Institute of International Education and one of the first members of the school's board, pointed out "that in this day of irritating propaganda few enterprises can be more gratifying to an intelligent American than an activity such as the Lycée Français de New York."[181] Dr. Duggan goes on to insist that the only aim of the Lycée is "sound education," although the following comments show that he was also optimistic about the effect that the exchange between young French and American students could have on the future of

French-American relations:

> [The Lycée] offers the opportunity for an education simultaneously in two civilizations which have many elements in common. It would be difficult for a young American studying at the lycée not to develop an appreciation of the fine elements of French culture. It would be equally true that the young French boy or girl would absorb a respect and admiration for the best elements of American civilization. And neither would sacrifice any of his love for his own country. [182]

Thus, the Lycée adopted an international outlook from the very beginning, emphasizing the importance of the coexistence of French and American culture within the school's walls. Duggan's words also point to the possibility of cultural exchange, and even to the possibility of developing an affinity for French language and culture among the school's American students, despite the fact that the founders appear to have been skeptical about the ability of the school to appeal to American students. Similarly, Frank Pierrepont Graves, the New York State Commissioner of Education and an early supporter of the school, compared the LFNY to the State University of New York, an institution which had been founded two centuries previously and which, like the new Lycée, had been inspired by the French model of education: in this way, the Lycée and the State University were like "mother and daughter" with a common purpose and a common history.[183]

To help organize the new school, de Fontnouvelle set up two committees to form the core of the school's governing body. One was primarily made up of university educators, most of whom were of French origin and had themselves been educated in France, including representatives from Hunter College, Barnard College, Columbia University, Harvard and the City College. The second committee consisted of American businessmen, lawyers and educators including university presidents and an associate superintendent of New York City Schools. Notable board members included Forsyth Wickes, a lawyer and a member of the board of directors of Shell Oil Company; Frank Pierrepont Graves, the Commissioner of Education of the State of New York; Jacob Greenberg, the adjunct superintendent of schools in New York City; and Nicholas Murray Butler, the

President of Columbia University. [184] This strategy of recruiting influential public figures from both the United States and France to serve on the school's board and thereby legitimizing the mission of the school closely resembles the strategy adopted by Hyde de Neuville to help found the Economical School over one hundred years earlier.[185]

De Fontnouvelle and the two committees recruited a core group of teachers in the spring and summer of 1935, one of whom, Pierre Brodin, was to remain for a career of over 41 years as Director of Studies. All of them apparently agreed to work for modest salaries (or even as volunteers) during the first year. Four of these teachers were assigned by the French Ministry of National Education to teach at the Lycée for a limited period, a practice known as *détachement*.[186]

The Lycée officially opened in October 1935 in three classrooms loaned by and later rented from the French Institute at 22 E 60th Street. [187] It was chartered by the Board of Regents of the State University of New York. Twenty-four students formed three classes, including grades 2, 4 and 6. Most were French or of French origin, including three of de Fontnouvelle's own children. The curriculum followed the official French program of studies with the addition of compulsory English for all students and compulsory Latin for the 6th grade. This ability to deliver the official French program in French was remarkable and the Lycée became the first school in New York to be permitted to administer a primarily foreign curriculum.

The acquisition of a substantial mansion on East 95th Street in 1937 was an important milestone for the school. Purchased for the relatively low sum of $135,000, the building guaranteed a secure future for the school.[188] According to Dubosclard, the Lycée received substantial financial support from the French government in its early years, in large part to help finance the purchase of this building. In the first two years of the school's existence, the *Service des Oeuvres* paid the salaries of two teachers assigned by the French Ministry of National Education, and helped to pay down the debt that the school had assumed to purchase its new buildings. In 1942, the French Consulate in New York agreed to pay the newly created Lycée an annual sum of $12,000. [189] By Dubosclard's calculation, this represented 20% of the school's operational costs. Another $48,000 per year was assigned to help pay down the school's debt, in addition to the support offered by the *Service des Oeuvres* mentioned above. Finally, beginning in 1938-1939 the French Ministry of National Education awarded the Lycée an annual sum of 75,000 francs to help provide scholarships to students who could not afford the school's tuition; according to Dubosclard, this group amounted to about one-third of the student body, or about forty students.[190] The rest of the school's budget was pieced together from private donations from the French expatriate community in New York City.[191]

De Fontnouvelle's initiative was truly innovative. Indeed, the idea of a bilingual and bicultural education was fairly new at the time, especially in the United States. While many bilingual schools had existed in the United States, especially German schools, they rarely incorporated any aspects of foreign curricula. In the Midwest especially there were thousands of students in private, parochial and even public schools studying in German. However, despite the strong interest by German-speaking immigrants in the rigorous Prussian education system and the German language, these schools were generally adaptations, using the German language while promoting an American curriculum. Moreover, the German schools largely disappeared following the United States' entry into World War I.[192] The Lycée would be quite different, adapting to American governance and financial needs while ensuring an education that not only adopted French as the language of instruction, but also the French curriculum and therefore the "universal" French values at its heart. One *New York Times* article from June 1936—one year after the school's founding—describes the Lycée as a "test school" and praises the success of the "experiment."[193]

While the school was accredited by the French Ministry of National Education, its curriculum differed in several ways from what one would expect in a Lycée in France. From the very beginning, the curriculum was a combination of French and of American offerings, making the LFNY a truly bilingual and bicultural institution, even while favoring French for most instruction. In 1936, Dr. Stephen Duggan, the President of the Institute of International Education and a pioneer in the field of international education, put it in the following way:

The Lycée Français de New York [...] has elements in its curriculum additional to those found in the Lycée in France. Much attention is given to physical training, music and extracurricular activities. English, American and English literature and American history and civics occupy an important place. Plays and dances are not overlooked as in the lycées in France. Visits are made to museums.[194] According to Dr. Duggan, parents and visitors were enthusiastic about the results, demonstrating the "wisdom of the experiment" and the Lycée's complete success in offering "an education in two civilizations."[195]

During the following years, more classes were added, and in 1939, the State of New York granted the school a permanent charter which permitted it to deliver the same instruction as that offered in any classical Lycée in France. Paul Hazard, a professor at the College de France and an inspector from the French Ministry of National Education, visited the Lycée in 1942 and delivered the following report: "I inspected the classes, questioned the students, met the teachers: my overall impression is excellent. Devoted teachers deliver their classes methodically and with authority; the level of instruction is as good as in our schools in France."[196]

In 1940 the first group of candidates was presented for the French baccalaureate exam.[197] Because of wartime conditions in Europe, the graduating class was larger than expected, and included several students who were refugees from France hoping to complete their studies in New York. The examining board included French professors who had been taken in by American universities as they fled from occupied Europe, as well as professors from academic departments at Columbia University, Princeton University, and the Rockefeller Institute of Medical Research.[198]

World War II

The first major challenge that the school faced came with France's declaration of War against Germany in September 1939. Following the outbreak of the war in 1939, several teachers returned immediately to serve in the French military, and after General de Gaulle's famous speech on 18 June 1940 denouncing the proposed armistice with Nazi Germany and calling for "all Frenchmen who want to remain free" to rally, a number of upper school students, both boys and girls, enlisted in the Free French Forces or in the armies of England, Holland and Norway. Ultimately eight former students from those classes died during the war, including Charles de Fontnouvelle, son of the school's founder.[199]

The Lycée had already been an important space for continuing Franco-American cooperation as the situation in Europe deteriorated. After Hitler annexed Austria in March 1938, President Roosevelt made it clear that the United States intended to remain neutral, even in the event of the invasion of Czechoslovakia.[200] In April 1938—just one month after the annexation of Austria—Dr. Nicholas Murray Butler, the president of Columbia University, and the Count René Doynel de Saint-Quentin, the French Ambassador to the United States, delivered a joint address at the Lycée to commemorate the intellectual bonds between France and the United States, hinting at an effort to strengthen French-American relations as the diplomatic situation worsened in Europe. In his speech, Dr. Butler "traced the long history of French-American relations and pointed out the many strikingly parallel thoughts and actions of Frenchmen and Americans in their eighteenth century revolutions, their first educational systems and their enunciation and practice of the principles of democracy."[201] The following comments make the political implications of such a sentiment clear, especially within the context of the system of alliances and the rise of fascism in pre-war Europe: "Those ideas of liberty, equality and fraternity honored here and in France and Great Britain are now held in common by no other nation in the world. It is a union of intellectual and moral terms and is one making not only for the happiness but for the progress of mankind."[202] The role of the Lycée as a space for Franco-American cooperation in the years before the United States entered the war in Europe was confirmed by Ambassador Saint-Quentin, who described the school as a "national asset" to France,[203] emphasizing the role of the school in France's cultural diplomacy during that period.

The community of French diplomats and expatriates in the United States were hardly united however in their visions for France's future. George Steiner, a literary critic and philosopher as well as an alumnus of the LFNY, chronicles these difficult years in his autobiography. He writes: "during the war years, the French *Lycée* in Manhattan was a cauldron."[204] Steiner attributes this at least in part to the tensions that existed between the different communities that the Lycée served at the time. Indeed, it was during this period that the Lycée saw a large influx of refugees fleeing occupied Europe, including both students who were able to continue their studies in New York thanks to the substantial scholarships awarded by the school as well as teachers who were willing to fill the vacancies created by the wartime enlistment of several members of the Lycée's French faculty.[205] According to Steiner, "the sons and daughters of diplomats, colonial servants, and military personnel loyal to the Vichy regime mingled with the children of exiles, of Jewish refugees, and of European families variously stranded in the New World."[206] The internal division within the Lycée's population is confirmed by Stephan Haimo, the current Chairman of the Board of the Lycée: "During the war, there were two camps at the Lycée. There was a Gaullist camp and a Pétainist camp."[207] Indeed, although official records during this period are sparse, Steiner's view is that during these years, "the official line [at the Lycée] was collaborationist."[208] However, by the end of the war the tide seems to have shifted: "The winds veered with cynical abruptness. I recall the morning on which a Cross of Lorraine, strictly banned hitherto, made its opportune appearance on the assembly-room wall. The 'Marseillaise' was intoned at full throat."[209]

During the Vichy era, New York City itself became a bastion of Free French intellectuals. One consequence of this is that the Cultural Services of the French Embassy to the United States have continued to be based in New York rather than in Washington, where all the other Embassy services are housed. Jean-Marie Guéhenno, the Cultural Councilor at the French Embassy in New York from 1982 to 1986, explains the situation in the following terms:

> It goes back to 1945. It's an anomaly really, which is related to the history of French-American cultural relations during World War II. At the time, the government of Pétain was recognized by the U.S. government, from [1940] until the operations in North Africa. Most of the Gaullists were in

New York, intellectuals who had fled France. There was a sense that Washington, in terms of culture, had been with Pétain. When the new French regime took over, the first Cultural Attaché was Claude Lévi-Strauss and there was no question that he should be in Washington. [210]

During this time, the Lycée was home to a large number of refugees from occupied Europe, and many faculty members were intellectuals and university professors who had fled France after the Maréchal Pétain's rise to power. As Naomi Schor, an alumnus of the Lycée who later became a professor of French at Yale University, wrote of the wartime years:

> The years I spent at the Lycée [...] are without a doubt what left the deepest imprint on my life because it was there that I discovered my vocation, the study of French literature, and found my native land. As a daughter of Polish-Jewish refugees reaching the United States in the midst of war after too short a stay in France, where my parents meant to settle, I found in the Lycée that lost homeland, a kind of first-aid citizenship. [211]

Quoted in a *New York Times* article dated May 10, 1942, Charles de Fontnouvelle voiced his hope that the cultural and political bonds that had linked the governments of France and the United States in the past would survive so long as "true French culture" survived in the United States, kept alive in institutions like the Lycée Français de New York: "So long as true French culture survives, there will always be a free interchange of ideas between the people of the two nations."[212]

In any case, many of the school's students were the children of refugees and French intellectuals opposed to the Vichy regime. For instance, Pierre Brodin, the school's Director of Studies from 1935 to 1976, joined a group of refugee intellectuals in founding the Free French University (École libre des hautes études) of New York in 1941, and was involved in teaching classes there throughout Germany's occupation of France. The institution was housed in the same building and shared some staff with the New School for Social Research, including the anthropologist and future Cultural Councilor

Claude Lévi-Strauss and the linguist Roman Jakobson. Like the Lycée, the Free French University served both expatriates and American students who wanted to immerse themselves in French culture, even after the war. It eventually tapered off into an occasional lecture series, of which Dr. Brodin served as a professor, dean and, finally, president.[213]

The school's history during the post-war period continued to reflect French-American relations and international affairs more generally. The war itself had brought a large number of refugees to the school, both teachers and students, and while some were to return to France, a number remained in New York. The incorporation of an exile community during the Second World War also mirrors the experience of the Economical School and the community of French refugees from Saint-Domingue.[214]

In the years following the war, other European refugees and immigrants from French-speaking countries increased the enrollment at the school. The creation of the Fulbright exchange program in 1946 opened the way for the recruitment of teachers from France who could work at the Lycée for up to three years on special visas without paying federal or state income tax, a substantial financial benefit for the school, which was able to hire teachers from France at relatively modest salaries. The opening of the United Nations Secretariat in New York in 1950 also led to a further increase in French speaking diplomatic families in New York and the process of decolonization and increase in United Nations member countries resulted in an increasingly diverse student body at the school, with children of most Francophone countries in attendance and even a position on the board of trustees reserved for an African representative.

The school met the needs of the expanded student body with the acquisition of new buildings; first the construction of a modest classroom building adjacent to the mansion at 95th Street (1958), then buildings on 72nd Street (1964), 93rd Street (1978) and on 73rd Street in 1996. The buildings at 72nd and 93rd also provided living space for the school's president, Maurice Galy, and future director of studies, Joel Vallat. Enrollment remained between 800 and 1,000 students. In 2002 these buildings would be sold to allow for the construction of a new facility on a single site (505 East 75th Street) which now houses nearly 1,300 students representing 50 nationalities.

Changes in Leadership and the Galy Years

De Fontenouvelle remained in New York after leaving the Consulate and stayed on as the president of the Lycée until his death in the spring of 1956. Robert Lacour-Gayet and Jean de Sieyès served as interim presidents for the next two years, before Maurice Galy (1918-1993), the adjunct cultural councilor of the Cultural Services of the French Embassy in New York, was appointed as the new head of school.[215] Galy would serve as the head of the Lycée for thirty-two years, from December 1957 to June 1989, during which time he led the school with what some have described as an authoritarian rule; Dubosclard writes the Galy set out the make the Lycée "his school."[216] The Lycée saw major growth and transformations under his tenure, including the acquisition of five new buildings to house the growing number of students who attended the school, from 285 in 1957 to nearly 1,000 in 1989.[217] In addition, Galy quickly increased the number of teachers at the school from twenty-nine in 1957, to fifty-five in 1960, to seventy in 1961. During the 1966-1967 school year, the Lycée's annual budget increased to one million dollars, with an enrollment of more than one thousand students and a staff of eighty-eight.[218]

Along with his wife Paule, Maurice Galy encouraged a tradition of lavish fundraisers to help support the school and cultivate its prestigious image, including a 1961 fundraising event for the school that featured a bazaar, a dancing party for teenagers, and a dinner dance for adults in the style of a "Grande Soirée de Gala."[219] According to Maristella Lorch, a former professor of Italian literature at Columbia University, as well as a former board member and parent of the Lycée Français, these events were an essential component of the school's success:

> You don't get money in America just by advertising on the paper. So [the Galys] decided to put up a kind of show that was the image of the ideal French school that didn't exist anymore in France... Galy had given [the Lycée] a good base. In order for a foreign school to succeed at that time, you

had to have those dances with all of the students dressed *à la* Louis XIV. [220]

In other words, the events not only served as fundraisers, but also created an image of the school based on an idealized version of European culture that appealed to an American audience. In many respects, what the Lycée offered was an idealized version of French education and French culture in New York, one that didn't necessarily correspond to the reality in France but which was nevertheless very appealing to elite Americans who were drawn to the prestige of French language and French culture.

During this period, the Lycée's student body also grew increasingly diverse, including students of more than forty different nationalities by 1965.[221] Galy made a concerted effort to recruit the families of African diplomats to the Lycée and appointed several of these new parents to the schools' board, including the ambassador from the Ivory Coast. Some members of the Lycée community, including Joel Vallat, a former director of studies at the school, have interpreted these actions as a strategic attempt to build a strong Francophone contingent within the school's student body and especially its board:

> I think [Galy's] appointments to the board were given to people whom he could trust and with whom he was friendly. He feared certain American members of the board whom he felt undermined his authority, and in my opinion, he was trying to build a group of loyal Francophones who would support him. [222]

These efforts to include more Francophones, however, did not enhance the Lycée's relationship with France.

According to French diplomat Jean-Marie Guéhenno, "the relationship with France was terrible... [they were] barely on speaking terms."[223] More than anything else, this falling out between the Lycée and the French government seems to have been a question of the personalities involved, particularly Maurice Galy's strong desire to manage the school after his own fashion. As Vallat explains, "Galy's personality did not tolerate meddling from French officials, since he was the head of an American school and he wanted to make the most of it... Galy refused to compromise."[224] One major source of tension was that despite its French curriculum, the Lycée was a private American school and therefore completely independent from the French authorities.

Maurice Galy himself explained that the originality of the Lycée Français was not the fact that it was a French-language institution—indeed, schools of this type had existed in the United States since the eighteenth century, as seen in the previous chapter—but rather the conditions under which the school was created and developed. According to Galy, there were two main obstacles to surmount. Firstly, the school needed to raise enough money to finance itself. Secondly, and perhaps more importantly, the Lycée needed to convince the American authorities to allow the school to follow the French, that is to say foreign, curriculum.[225] Galy also explained that the private status of the Lycée was shocking to many in France who were accustomed to the country's public school system:

> The combination of a private business corporation with an educational establishment was shocking to many of our countrymen, notably teaching professionals or public sector employees. They cringed when I happily told them that my responsibilities included the management of a portfolio of financial assets, real estate investment, fundraising and turning a profit on events such as dinners and benefit galas, as well as the selling of textbooks and school supplies.[226]

This sometimes led to severe disagreement between the administration of the school, represented by Galy, and French education officials. Indeed, as Galy explains, the French government never gave up on the idea that school was under their control:

> This explains in part why the [the Lycée's] status as an American private school was never really acknowledged by the French administration, even if they always recognized the very high quality of the education there. [The administration] always dreamed of exercising their direct control over the school's administration, its management, its curriculum, and the hiring of teachers... This created conflicts that made our job difficult and continue to do so.[227]

Another particularly tense episode that illustrates the difficulty of the relationship between the Lycée and the French authorities was the attempt by some of the faculty to form a teacher's union in 1981, an episode which will be recounted in greater detail below.

An Uneasy Relationship with France:
The Labor Dispute of 1981

Motivated by the election of President Mitterrand and his left-wing government in 1981, several French teachers at the Lycée decided to unionize. These teachers also had the support of the Cultural Counselor at the time, André-Jean Libourel, who was known to be left-leaning. According to Vallat, the Director of Studies at the Lycée between 1974 and 1982, the labor dispute was at the source of a series of major misunderstandings between French officials and the Lycée administration that "quickly turned political."[228] For example, many of teachers who had left France, either temporarily or on more permanent exchange visas, were very happy to be in New York, but then discovered that they were in a private American school and were displeased with the private system in which teachers and parents had little voice in the organization of the school.

According to Vallat, the situation quickly became tense because Maurice Galy, the President of the Lycée, refused to compromise:

> He was very hostile to these teachers from France who wanted to change his way of doing things. It was very complicated, and for him it was the beginning of a difficult period. I don't know if these tensions between the Lycée and the Consulate or the Embassy existed before the rise of the Left in 1981. I think it was a question of the personalities involved as well as the political climate in France. [229]

The faculty representatives garnered the support of the New York State United Teachers chapter of the AFL-CIO American Federation of United Teachers which sponsored an election for the right to unionize in 1983. After achieving an initial victory, the union was then challenged by Galy and school's board, leading to an appeal to the National Labor Relations Board. Ultimately the NLRB ruled that there could be no bargaining unit in the school because of the very different statuses governing the hiring and working conditions of

French teachers and local hires.

In 1985, the Lycée employed about eighty-three teachers, thirteen school "monitors" or assistants, two library aides, and one laboratory technician. Of these, about half of the faculty and a few of the monitors and aides held exchange visas as visitors from France.[230] Like locally hired employees, these exchange visitors were hired by the president of the Lycée and shared some conditions of employment, receiving the same gross wages and sharing the same holidays, vacations, and work year as their locally hired colleagues. However, according to the decision of the NLRB cited above, there were "significant differences" in the employment conditions of the two groups.[231] For example, exchange visitors received a $2200 allowance to help offset the cost of relocation. More importantly, for the first two years of their three-year visas, exchange visitors were not subject to local, state or federal taxes. Moreover, exchange visitors from the Ministry of National Education who were granted official leave or *détachement* from the Ministry continued to be covered by their French health plan, and their years working at the Lycée were counted towards their pension and seniority status in France. Exchange visitors were also evaluated by inspectors from the Ministry of National Education, as required to gain seniority in the French civil service and in a process completely separate from the Lycée's internal evaluation procedures. These differences are summarized by a 1983 decision of the NLRB, which rules that "the French exchange teachers employed by the private school should not be included in the bargaining unit with the locally hired teachers":

> [The Board] found that the interests of the exchange teachers diverged from those of the locally hired employees in several different ways. It pointed out, among other things, that the salaries of the exchange visitors are not subjected to United States taxes for two years, which is as long as most visitors stay; the visitors have their own pension and health plans; their time at the Lycée is credited to their pension and seniority status in France; and most of the exchange visitors come from the French Ministry of Education and, thus, their contracts, hours, and work performance are subject to standards of the Ministry. [232]

In the end, the Board concluded that "the instances where the interests of the exchange visitors diverged from or were in conflict with those of the locally hired employees were fundamental and outweighed the instances of shared concerns which the Regional Director had relied on in including visiting teachers in the bargaining unit"[233]. In addition, the divergence of interests between local hires and French exchange teachers was not limited to the terms of the contracts or the conditions under which they were hired, and is in fact representative of a cultural divide between the French-speaking and the American-speaking teachers at the school. Although this is not explicitly mentioned in the NLRB decision, French teachers had very little to do with their American counterparts, mostly due to the fact that during this period there were only a very small number of American teachers at the school and their responsibilities were limited to teaching English classes. Their schedules often did not overlap, and English classes were largely seen as separate from the school's mostly French curriculum.[234]

The dispute over the unionization had a significant impact on the school, both financially and culturally. The Ministry of Education, the AEFE, or the Ministry of Foreign Affairs withdrew the Lycée's right to *détachement*. This was a major blow since the school relied on these teachers who were part of the Ministry of Education and who cost the school much less than local hires.

This episode illustrates the mounting tensions as the school in New York asserted its independence from the French authorities. The French government's response to these and other small crises would be to strengthen, centralize, and standardize its international network of schools, ultimately leading to the creation of the Agency for French Education Abroad (Agence pour l'enseignement français à l'étranger or AEFE).[235]

The Student Body and Curriculum

The student body of the LFNY has historically been very diverse, but broadly speaking can be broken into three groups, each with their own rationale for attending the school. Joel Vallat, the former assistant director of the LFNY and the longtime head of the Lycée Louis-le-Grand in Paris, explains this dynamic in further detail:

> The school's population could be split into three categories: one-third French, one-third Americans, and one-third other nationalities, including U.N. diplomats as well as executives, bankers, engineers who came to New York for a few years, since New York was the financial capital of the United States. Each category of the school's population had very different reasons to be there. [236]

The population of French students could be further divided into two sub-categories based on whether their families intended to establish themselves in the United States or to return to France. Vallat continues:

> For the French people who only planned on spending a couple of years in New York, the Lycée was temporary, since they planned on finishing high school in France. Those that stayed longer, on the other hand [...] wanted to go to American universities. [237]

In other words, the French population was split between those who planned on returning to France and therefore saw the Lycée as a good way to continue their education with the intent of reintegrating into the French public school system upon their return. The other category saw the Lycée as a way to maintain their French language and culture, although they fully intended to remain in the United States after their graduation from the school. As already noted, the French baccalaureate diploma already permitted Lycée graduates to be admitted with advanced standing to most American colleges and universities. In fact, the State of New York recognized the rigorous curriculum of the high school program by allowing the LFNY to issue the New York high school diplomas after 11th grade, rather than after 12th grade as in most other schools.

The second third of the student body includes Americans and binational families. For these families, the Lycée was an attractive school because it would allow their children to have a dual education as Americans with a French educational background. As described above, the reasons for attending the Lycée were fairly self-evident for French nationals, namely to maintain their children's French language and culture as well as the possibility of reintegrating the

French school system upon their eventual return to France. The same is true for international or highly mobile families, who were drawn by the fact that French schools can be found around the world, thereby guaranteeing the continuity of their children's education. For American families, however, the reasons for attending the Lycée are more diverse. Indeed, many American families with children enrolled in the Lycée had no immediate family connection to France or to the French language. Many families were nevertheless drawn to the Lycée by the status of the French language, the perceived rigor and intellectual orientation of the French secondary school system, and the prestige of the Lycée among private schools in New York City, as well as a growing interest in bilingual education in more recent years. As Fabrice Jaumont, the Education Attaché at the French Embassy to the United States in New York, wrote in his response to the survey, "American families were either interested in the experience of bilingualism [or] for the perceived rigor of the French educational standards". Each of these reasons will be discussed in greater detail below.

The interest in French language and French culture is probably the single most common reason American families have for sending their children to the Lycée, even if they have no immediate personal or family connection to France. For example, many parents enrolled their children in the Lycée because they believed in the benefits of bilingual education. Don Zivkovic, a former board member and a parent at the Lycée between 1989 and 2000, explains that he and his wife, who are both Australian citizens, chose the Lycée for their children "because we wanted our children to be raised bilingual [...] and there was a bi-cultural aspect to it, which was a benefit as well."[238]

Parents were also drawn to the rigorous pedagogy of the French school system. As Zivkovic explains, "there was an attitude towards rote learning that we admired."[239] Vallat agrees with this assessment, arguing that American families were drawn to the perceived rigor of the French system and the high quality of the education dispensed at the Lycée, as well as the high status of French language and culture:

There were American members of the New York intelligentsia, like university professors and *New York Times* journalists, who weren't bilingual but who were interested in France and knew of the rich academic offerings of the French secondary school system. [These parents believed] that a French student who graduates from high school has received a superior cultural and scientific education to that of someone who went through the American system, even at a good school... They valued the high academic standards and favored cultural development over the kind of personal growth that you would see in an Anglo-Saxon school, particularly in the United States. [240]

This statement is confirmed by the experience of American students at the Lycée, like one survey respondent who reported that the academic discipline that the French system had instilled in her would continue to serve her throughout her life: "From my French language teachers, I learned that rigor is the path to quality results. From the French directors of the school, I learned that effort only pays off if it is defended with pride and loyalty" . Similarly, many students found that the Lycée was an excellent preparation for higher education, on par with or perhaps even exceeding American schools, as described by Mira Schor in her response to the survey:

I appreciated [the value of the French system] the minute I hit American education in college—my best friend's A papers at NYU seemed incredibly poorly organized to me, coming from the rigid structure imposed on us by the French system and I really came to appreciate the discipline and rules almost immediately.

While the rigor of the curriculum and the disciplined approach of the professors, mostly recruited from France, appealed to families seeking both bilingualism and intellectual stimulation for their children, there have always been additional reasons for non-French families to choose the Lycée.

Then, as now, there is a certain status associated with the French language and French culture, as well as the fact of attending a highly-regarded private school on the Upper East Side. This was felt by children as well as by parents, and former students also report the feeling of distinctiveness that came along with speaking French with classmates on the streets of New York: "Once we were in the upper grades and [...] could take the bus home, we were very distinctive because we spoke French, so people could tell who we were and where we were coming from."[241] Other survey respondents reported that the fact that they attended the Lycée granted them a feeling of "special status" among their English-speaking peers.

The prestigious image of the Lycée has been maintained throughout its history, beginning with high-profile events organized by the founder of the school, Charles de Fontnouvelle, such as a 1936 charity concert at Carnegie Hall including a performance by the French-American opera singer Lily Pons that was put on to aid the endowment of the school. The event was attended by André Lefebvre de Labouaye, the French Ambassador to the United States; Jesse Isidor Straus, the United States Ambassador to France; and the mother of President Franklin Roosevelt. [242] Other such events included a 300-person dedication ceremony to celebrate the school's move to a new building in 1938 in the "beautifully paneled ballroom" of the Lycée, preceded by dinner party in the Louis XVI suite of the Saint Regis Hotel that was attended by several important dignitaries and high society figures, including the mother of the President, Mrs. James Roosevelt.[243]

Many American students had no trouble keeping pace with the French peers in the Francophone environment of the Lycée. According to former parents and students, American and other non-French students were able to quickly adapt to the French language and curriculum. Zivkovic explains that "it was very simple... within six months, [my daughter] was fluent."[244] For others, the transition was more difficult, particularly in terms of adapting to the culture of the school. Michele Moss, an American alumnus of the Lycée Français who spoke almost no French when she first arrived at the school, tells one such story:

> I had gotten a 0 on a math test because the teacher had described a straight line as "*l'aspect que prend un fil bien tendu*," and I understood it to be "*la direction que prend une fille bien connue*," because I thought *connue* was the same thing as "smart," and so a smart girl would go in a straight line. So that's what I wrote on my *interrogation écrite*, so of course the teacher gave me a 0 and I burst out crying. It's a memory of how little I understood when I first arrived![245]

While many adapted to the rigor and intellectual focus of the school even with difficult transitions, some students, including artist Mira Schor, felt that ultimately the Lycée curriculum suffered from a certain rigidity, making it difficult to explore alternative forms of enrichment such as art or music; indeed, over the course of the school's history many students have left the Lycée before their final year seeking a more flexible educational environment.[246]

The third group is very heterogeneous and includes a mix of highly mobile professionals and diplomats from around the world. As Vallat explains, these families were drawn to the Lycée because it belonged to the international network of French schools, which guaranteed the continuity of their children's education.

> The third group included students of over 50 nationalities who chose to study at the Lycée Français. This was in large part due to the influx of diplomats and executives in New York, people with jobs that required them to move from country to country... For these parents, who were very international and who moved from country to country every few years, the system [of international French schools] was very convenient.... No matter where they were coming from and no matter where they were sent, they knew that there would be a Lycée Français.[247]

This appeal to an international elite was, of course, central to the purpose of the creation of the network of French schools.

Cultural Identity of the
Lycée Français de New York

The cultural identity of the LFNY has shifted considerably over the years. For many, the Lycée was a "citadel" of French culture in New York City, as described by Don Zivkovic.[248] Students studied an exclusively French curriculum including French literature, French geography, and French history, and were expected to sing the *Marseillaise*, although from the beginning there were concessions to the New York State rules and regulations governing school curricula, including for example obligatory hours of instruction in English, American history, and even for a short time the history of the State of New York.[249] The Star Spangled Banner and the American Flag also shared the stage during official school events. Unlike today's current practices, where instruction at the Lycée is conducted in French and in English in several disciplines including math and science, during the 1950s and through the 1980s all classes at the Lycée were taught in French with the exception of English language and literature classes and the limited hours of American history at some grade levels.

The French curriculum had a significant impact on the cultural identity of students, particularly Americans at the Lycée who often felt that they developed a "French identity" despite not having a personal or a family connection to France or to French culture. Mira Schor, a student at the Lycée between 1955 and 1967, said that being at the Lycée at that time "was like being in France in New York."[250] In her survey response, Schor pointed to courses in French literature and philosophy courses as important cornerstones in her intellectual and cultural development: "For me it remained as an important intellectual formation, understanding as time passed how much I had been steeped in Enlightenment thought... I think that the literary and philosophical education I received was very useful to me as an intellectual foundation."[251] Another survey respondent expressed a similar opinion, writing that "the program is truly a French one, focusing on French history, and literature," with the ultimate result being that all the students, both French and American, "grow up feeling French." Indeed, some students were so immersed in French language and French culture that they at times may have felt more of an affinity to France than to their country, as recounted in this anecdote from 1970s, Columbia University Professor Maristella Lorch who was a parent and a long time Trustee: "My daughters looked out the window and they said, 'The Loire this morning is in bad shape,' but it happened to be the Hudson. They didn't even know that we lived in New York!"[252]

Several survey respondents pointed out that the strong French identity of the Lycée was important since it was surrounded by the American culture of New York City and, more generally speaking, of the United States. As one respondent puts it, "the identification with French culture was very strong... American culture was an afterthought, but I didn't mind that, it was quite possible to pick up all the necessary information elsewhere."

Other survey respondents emphasized the international or global identity of the Lycée, especially in later years. One alumnus who attended the school between 1966 and 1980 wrote:

> The school fostered more of an international identity than a French or an American one. While there was access to French cultural events that came through New York City [...] the student body was so international—French-speaking Asian, North African, Italian—that we all felt mixed.

Similarly, one survey respondent acknowledged that although the curriculum put a strong emphasis on the French language and culture, the fact that the Lycée offered courses in American history, literature, and geography enabled students to graduate with an international perspective: "the latter, added to the multicultural composition of the student body, fosters a feeling of international identity and multiculturalism." In the end, it seems that students developed several identities in parallel, producing an international and global culture within the school, and that the French and American identities of students were able to exist side by side, with many enriching opportunities for exchange. For example, these comments made by Adam Zivkovic, a student at the Lycée between 1996 and 2010, seem to echo the hopes of founding board member Stephen Duggan:

Neither the French nor the Americans are particularly shy about their opinions, though they certainly voice them differently. One cannot really help walking away from a French school without picking up some of their values, as one could not really walk away from an American school with picking up some of theirs. The viewpoints are built into the experience, and certainly informed by the teachers. A very interesting time to be at the Lycée was always during an election—French or American. Discussion abounded on both sides, and it was especially interesting to see how deeply people cared about certain elections they could not even vote in, since some were French citizens but lived in the US, and so the outcomes affected them all the same.

Like many other survey respondents, Zivkovic concludes that this coexistence of cultures and identities produced students who were international and multicultural, or to use his words, "citizens of the world." Alain Letort, who was a student at the Lycée between 1951 and 1965, writes that the fact that all subjects were taught in French using French textbooks, except for English literature and American history, contributed to his "dual identity" as a Franco-American. He also adds that the diversity of the student body broadened his outlook: "many of my classmates were neither French nor American, so very early in life I developed a sense of being a citizen of the world." Letort also argues that the international faculty played an important part in developing the global culture of the school, as well as fostering a sense of mutual respect between children of different culture: "the French faculty transmitted French values, the U.S. faculty transmitted American values, but all were very conscious that the student body was international and taught us to respect each other's cultures."

Fundraising and Institutional Support

Over its more than eighty-year history, the Lycée Français has sometimes benefited from the support of the French government, and other times been sustained by the local French-speaking community with very little support from France. Indeed, according to parent Don Zivkovic, in later years the French government's financial support of the Lycée was minimal, especially when it came to the expansion of the school and the construction of the new building. He contrasts the French attitude with the American approach to fundraising and the United States government's support for American schools in France:

> The American School in Paris was very strongly supported by Americans in Paris, the American government, American corporations... What we experienced was the exact opposite. We got help from Americans, but very little help from the French. I sat in on meetings [...] with French corporation, and they didn't [...] seem to be interested in getting involved.[253]

Joelle Reilly, a teacher at the Lycée, confirms this feeling that the French government was never very interested in supporting the Lycée financially, claiming that "the French government was never extremely generous."[254]

Despite pressure from the French government to keep tuition at the Lycée low in order to provide an affordable education to French families living abroad, the cost of attending the school has increased considerably over the years. Moreover, although the bylaws of the AEFE require the French government to provide financial aid to French families attending the school, the amount of aid available is severely limited by budgetary constraints. Instead, the Lycée has had to support itself through its own American-style fundraising and tuition, the success of which currently has enabled the school to sustain a more generous scholarship program than in the past:

> The school offers a lot more scholarship money now... They do fundraising. They've bought into that part of the head [of school]'s job and that part of a community's need, which is to raise money and grow that money in a healthy way, and redistribute a portion of it to families to offset the cost of tuition, which has gone up considerably, and to pay for the teachers. [255]

The tuition is need-based and all families are eligible, although French families are required to apply for financial aid through the Consulate first. The scholarships offered by the Lycée cover up to 95% of tuition, never the full cost, in order to give families a sense of ownership in the school. As Reilly explains, "[the head of school] said that he never wanted to give 100% because he felt it was important that everybody be symbolically part of the school that way. Even if it's just 5%, you should be a little bit a part of that."[256]

Growth of the French Population and Other French Schools in New York

From the mid-1950s through the 1970s, the French expatriate community in New York grew, and with it there was a growing demand for French instruction and for admission to the Lycée, which during this period purchased additional buildings on the Upper East Side of Manhattan to accommodate them, as noted above.

This growth also presented opportunities for other French schools, including the Fleming School (founded in 1956), The Lyceum Kennedy (founded in 1964) and the French American School of New York (founded in 1980). All three were founded by the former teachers from the Lycée Français. Another French-American school, the École Internationale de New York, opened its doors in 2009 and was founded by the former head of the Lyceum Kennedy. In order to provide additional context for the expansion of French education in New York over the past sixty years, the history and present status of each of these schools will be described in detail in the pages that follow.

The Fleming School was founded in 1956 by Douce Fleming Correa, a teacher at the LFNY who sought to provide an alternative to the more strictly French curriculum of the Lycée. Like the Lycée Français, the Fleming School existed to provide a blend of French and American education, with a strong focus on bilingualism, especially among the American students: according to Correa, "it is very important that American children should be bilingual." The Fleming School was initially located on East 62nd Street, before moving to new buildings on 78th and 79th Streets in 1990.

The Fleming School attracted a similar student body to that of the Lycée Français de New York, but appealed especially to families seeking a more American approach to education. One survey respondent wrote that "the school was essentially Franco-American in outlook... some of the students were French nationals, but more were American kids from liberal, educated families." The schools also attracted families for many of the same reasons. On the French side, "some of the students were there because they had French family histories, or even two French parents." For Americans, however, the reasons for attending the Fleming School were more nuanced: "I think most of us were there because our American parents wanted us to provide us with a broader cultural outlook and a better knowledge of western European culture in particular. Many of them were Francophiles who wanted to impart their enthusiasm to us" . Another survey respondent reports a similar story: "My family chose to enroll me to expose me to the French language from an early age and to teach me about French culture" . Yet another survey respondent reported a similar set of motivations:

> My parents, and some of my friends' parents, chose it because they felt that learning French was a valuable way to provide their children with some cultural polish, as well as to expose them to aspects of the western European canon that they might not otherwise have experienced.

Other alumni of the Fleming School cited the "cachet" of attending a French school, as well as the fact that the Fleming School, like the Lycée, was more affordable than other private schools in the area.

On the other hand, the somewhat bohemian culture of the Fleming School stood in stark contrast with the more traditional Lycée. One alumnus, Marcea Barringer, explains in her survey response that "most of the French kids in the school seemed to have been kicked out of the Lycée Français or had parents who were very unconventional [...] and for whom the Lycée did not seem like a good fit."

One survey respondent reported that the Fleming School fostered a bi-national sense of identity:

> We learned everything in two languages and we learned about two cultures. I remember learning the French alphabet along with the English alphabet. I remember learning penmanship in both French and English. I also remember having to curtsy in front of the headmistress and other customs that were more French than American.

Many former students emphasized the school's traditional French curriculum, which like the Lycée's emphasized traditional pedagogical methods such as rote memorization, rigor, and discipline:

> Much of the curriculum had a more European-oriented pedagogy, based on memorization of poetry, grammar, and facts. One thing that I recall and that benefited me immensely in coming years: when most schools were much more free-spirited with their curriculum, Fleming focused on the basics. We learned grammar, punctuation, and penmanship; our math curriculum was also very memory-focused.

Others recall that the curriculum was more flexible, integrating an American interest in self-expression and academic enrichment with the rigor of the French system:

> I think the French sense of discipline, order and respect [were] the values that I learned best. At the same time, there was a lot of room for creativity that seemed more "American," such as an emphasis on art, a wonderful modern dance program through third grade, and a marvelous chorus in 4th through 8th grades.

Like the Lycée, American alumni of the Fleming School developed a lifelong attachment to the French language and French culture, and perhaps even a sense of identity, even if that may not have been the school's intention. One survey respondent explained the transfer of French values in the following way:

> As a child, it did not seem that Fleming school actively worked to foster a sense of French culture in American students. However, since so many of the teachers at the school were French, other students were French, and many of our textbooks were French, some of it seeped in.

In this way, the Fleming School functioned in a manner very similar to the LFNY, spreading French language and culture to an ever-greater number of American students and providing a French education to those French students who were unable to find their place in the Lycée.

Unfortunately, the school's finances foundered, and the Fleming School was forced to close its doors midway through the school year in 1991 when a real estate transfer of the school's old buildings on 69th Street failed to raise the capital to refinance the new West Side complex. It is notable that the alumni of the Fleming School have continued to maintain their own Facebook page despite the disappearance of their alma mater more than twenty years ago.

The Lyceum Kennedy was founded in 1964 by Éliane Dumas. Like the founder of the Fleming school, Dumas had previously been employed as a teacher at the Lycée Français. The school was and still is located in midtown Manhattan, and like the LFNY was meant to serve the needs of French and francophone families living in New York. In 1986, the school was bought by a Japanese linguist named Koji Sonoda, who expanded the school's offering to include an English-Japanese as well as an English-French dual-language program. In 1996, the school opened a second campus in Westchester County to accommodate its growing population.

Today, the Lyceum Kennedy serves students from preschool to grade 12 and is accredited by the French Ministry of Education, as well as by the New York State Board of Regents. In September 2014, the Lyceum Kennedy gained recognition from the International Baccalaureate Organization (IBO) and inaugurated its IB Diploma Program.

The French-American School of New York (FASNY) was founded in 1980 by two former teachers from the LFNY, Katherine Watkins and Sylvette Maschino. The school was initially located in Larchmont, NY and started off with only 17 students in nursery school and pre-K. Since then, the school has grown to educate more than 800 students from pre-K to grade 12 every year. The school has several campuses in Westchester County and is currently working to build a state-of-the-art new facility in White Plains on the former site of the Ridgeway Country Club. FASNY serves a diverse and international population, and according to the school's website, 69% of the students are of French origin, 21% are American, and 10% represent fifty different nationalities.

Like the LFNY, the Fleming School, and the Lyceum Kennedy, FASNY is accredited by the French Ministry of Education, the International Baccalaureate Organization, and the New York State Association for Independent Schools. It is the only school in the New York metropolitan area accredited to offer both the International Baccalaureate and the French Baccalaureate, and all students also graduate with a New York State High School Diploma. According to one board member, "one differentiating factor for FASNY is that it is truly a dual curriculum and a dual language [school], with an international community." The school strives to combine the best elements of the French and the American educational systems through its "dual curriculum", and because of this the school appeals especially to multicultural households, or expats who also want English language and a more American experience for their children.

Finally, the École Internationale de New York was founded in 2009 by Yves Rivaud, the former head of the Lyceum Kennedy. The school is located in the Flatiron district in New York and currently serves students from pre-K through 8th grade. As of 2011, the school has around 16 to 18 students in each grade. The École Internationale de New York is accredited by the French Ministry of Education and is affiliated with the Mission laïque française, as well as the National Association for Independent Schools and the Parents League of New York.

Like the other schools discussed in this chapter, the École Internationale de New York, serves three main groups. The first of these includes French families living in New York, since the school follows a curriculum similar to the one taught in France with the addition of the "creative and critical approach of American education."[257] The second group includes American families who want their children to learn French through the school's immersion program. Finally, there are international families living and New York who are drawn to the school's "international vision," representing more than thirty different countries from around the world.[258]

Like the Fleming school, the École International de New York advertises itself as a dual curriculum as well as a dual language school, "artfully [blending] the best of the American and the French educational systems."[259]

Like the labor dispute, the emergence of new French schools in New York created an important motivation for the French government to standardize and centralize its expanding network of schools abroad, as will be discussed more fully in the following chapter.

CHAPTER VI

The View from Paris & the Agency for French Education Abroad

I began my career at the Lycée Français de New York teaching English classes in the elementary school and later shifted to middle school and then high school classes, teaching English and American history, both subjects required by the New York State Department of Education, and also clearly important for the large number of students who would continue their high school education in colleges and universities in the United States.

Initially as one of the few Americans on the faculty (even many of the other English teachers were French) I had very little to do with the French Ministry of Education. The other faculty members, regardless of the grades or subjects they taught, were all certified by the French government and subject to regular inspections as they advanced through French seniority ranks. These teachers received their curriculum guidelines in the weekly "*bulletins officiels*" (BO) from France, while the small group of American English teachers mostly relied on each other, and sometimes a department chair, to establish curriculum, usually with a nod to materials used in other private schools, or outlined in New York State standards, but without extensive input from other authorities. In the high school classes, we prepared students for SAT exams and helped with college applications in the United States, but the all-important Baccalaureate Examinations, even the English language tests, were exclusively the domain of the teachers who had been trained in France.

This changed in dramatically in 1998 when I was asked to coordinate a new program, the "International Option of the Baccalauréat" (OIB) at the Lycée, recruiting a group of students who would take special language and history-geography exams in English. I quickly learned that there were OIB "sections" in many other French Lycées around the world, not only in English (with both

American and British sections) but also in German, Arabic, Portuguese, Japanese and Swedish. In order to supervise the organization of the classes and the curriculum, I was plunged into multiple ministerial decrees, many updated "BO" announcements and, most interesting for me, new relationships with other schools both in the United States (Washington DC, Boston, Chicago, San Francisco) and in France where schools in Paris, Bordeaux, Lyons and Nice all offered "American Sections" for their English speaking students.

The last half of the twentieth century saw a significant growth in the French population in New York as well as the number of schools offering a fully French curriculum. In addition, well-established schools like the Lycée Français de New York were beginning to assert their independence from the French authorities, leading to a number of conflicts such as the labor dispute in 1980s and the growing tensions between head of school Maurice Galy and the French consular authorities in New York. These parallel developments were closely followed by the authorities back in France, especially within in the Ministry of National Education (Ministère de l'Éducation nationale) and the Ministry of Foreign Affairs (Ministère des affaires étrangères), and led to a series of decisions that would serve to centralize and standardize the rapidly expanding network of French schools abroad. This ongoing process of centralization and standardization ultimately led to the creation of the Agency for French Education Abroad (Agence pour l'enseignement français à l'étranger or AEFE) in 1990, which will be the primary subject of this chapter.

The successful growth and development of French schools in New York, even when launched by local philanthropists, parents, educators or other community members, was greatly facilitated by the fact that, even as private, independent schools, these schools benefited from the legitimacy of official recognition by the French authorities at the Ministry of Education and the Ministry of Foreign Affairs. The latter had a special interest in these schools, not only internationally, but also especially in New York where the United Nations as well as the international business community provided important potential for the "soft diplomacy" that could be accomplished through schools. Two French institutions, the French Lay Mission (Mission laïque française or MLF) and more recently the AEFE are largely responsible for oversight and for connecting the schools to the network and to the Ministries concerned. The support they offer, especially in curriculum, hiring of teachers, in service training and accreditation help distinguish these schools not only from other private schools in New York, but also from other privately franchised schools (like those that offer International Baccalaureate programs) or those that are more loosely associated (such as the Council of British Schools Overseas which is a membership organization of mainly private schools).

Today more than 490 French schools abroad receive administrative oversight (accreditation, appointment of teachers and administrators, curriculum approval and examinations) from the AEFE, created in 1990 by the Ministry of Foreign Affairs. The schools vary in their financial structures from entirely private (such as the Lycée Français de New York) to entirely public (primarily in developing countries, but also including long-established schools such as those in Berlin and Moscow). Additional schools continue to be created and supported by the MLF which enjoys special status as a French semi-governmental non-profit agency, and which currently administers 71 schools. The MLF provides support for creating French schools abroad in cooperation with the Ministry of National Education, the Ministry of Foreign Affairs and individual private corporations. While some of these schools are designed primarily to serve the French business community abroad, all of them include local students. This chapter will provide an overview of the present missions of these two organizations that assume the responsibility of administering the large network of French schools abroad, before delving into their organization and structure as well as a more detailed discussion of their activities in the United States and in New York in particular.

The French Lay Mission Today

The creation of the AEFE was greatly facilitated by the precedent set by the MLF, an organization with a long history of promoting and facilitation French education abroad.[260] The purpose, structure, and mission of the MLF has evolved considerably throughout its history, but today's charter states that its mission is to spread French language and culture throughout the world through education that is secular, multilingual, and multicultural. The central stated values of the MLF today are secularism, solidarity, and cultural exchange. The charter states explicitly that these values are derived from the Universal Declaration of the Rights of Man.[261] To realize its mission, the MLF works closely with the French Ministry of European and Foreign Affairs (MEAE) and the Ministry of National Education (MEN), as well as with the educational systems already in place in host countries and in the schools within the MLF network.

Today, the MLF is at the head of a network of 109 schools, which educate a total of more than 60,000 students in 38 different countries.[262] More than 71% of the students in the MLF network are foreign nationals.[263] This network includes elementary, middle, and high schools divided into four categories. In the first category, there are 35 schools that are directly administered by the MLF, known as "établissements en pleine responsabilité." The MLF directly manages the administrative, pedagogical, and financial responsibilities of these schools. Eight of these schools are jointly regulated by the AEFE, and one is jointly regulated by the Ministry of Foreign Affairs. The Dallas International School (DIS) in Texas, founded in 1984, is the only such school in the United States. The school was incorporated into the MLF network in 1991 and currently educates 725 children from preschool (*toute petite section*) to 12th grade (*terminale*). DIS follows the French national curriculum so that students graduating from middle school receive the French *diplôme national du brevet*, and students graduating from high school have the option of preparing either the French *baccaulauréat* (ES and S) or the International Baccalaureate. Most teachers at the school are certified by the French Ministry of National Education.

In the second category, there are 21 company schools, known as "écoles d'entreprise." These schools are created in response to requests made by companies wishing to facilitate the education of the children of their French-speaking employees at offshore facilities. Some examples of corporations that take advantage of this system are French firms such as Total, Bouygues, and Renault, but also international firms such as Comilog. The first company school was created in 1965 in Calgary, Canada to educate the children of workers at Elf Aquitaine. The number of company schools increased dramatically throughout the 1980s and 1990s, and in 2002 the MLF's company schools educated a total of 1,550 students per year.[264] The only MLF company school in the United States is the Areva School in Aiken, South Carolina. The school was created in 2006 at the request of expatriates working for Areva, a French multinational group specializing in nuclear power and renewable energy. The Areva School currently educates only nine students from 1st (CP) through 9th grade (3ème) and partners with three American schools in Aiken; all nine students are enrolled in an American school but take French classes taught by French teachers certified by the MEN and hired by the MLF.

In the third category, there are 53 partner schools, known as "établissements partenaires." These are schools that are legally and financially independent from the MLF but who wish to secure accreditation from the French Ministry of National Education through an agreement with the MLF. In practice, this means that the MLF is involved in the hiring of teachers and monitors the accreditation process and can play an advisory role in financial or administrative matters. There are currently 53 MLF partner schools in the United States, including one in New York, the International School of Brooklyn (ISB). Founded in 2005, ISB is a fully bilingual school with a French immersion program and was integrated into the MLF network in 2009. The school currently educates 167 students from Kindergarten (*maternelle*) to 8th grade (4ème), although for the moment the school is only accredited by the French MEN for K-3.

Finally, in the MLF leads 19 cooperative education missions ("missions de cooperation educative") in 9 countries at the behest of the Ministry of Foreign Affairs In these cases, the MLF is contracted by the French government to provide educational services in crisis or in post-crisis situations. For example, the MLF is responsible for two high schools in Kaboul, within the context of France's diplomatic mission in Afghanistan. There are currently two MLF missions in the United States, one in Florida and one in Washington. The French International School of Boca Raton in Florida and the North Seattle French School in Washington were both integrated into the MLF network in 2017.

The administration of the MLF is organized in three major bodies. The largest of these, the general assembly, meets twice per year and whenever else is called for by the President of the organization. The assembly approves expenses for the current fiscal year and votes on the following year's budget. The general assembly also elects 33 of 36 members of the governing board, the other three of whom are appointed by the Ministry of Foreign Affairs, the Ministry of National Education, and the AEFE. The board meets at least three times every six months and elects an eight-person bureau, which meets once per month. The MLF is based in Paris, from where it directs the oversight, the administration, and the development of its schools throughout the world.

According to the report on the future of French education abroad presented to the French government's Social and Economic Council in 2003, the MLF remains an essential partner of the AEFE in its mission to promote French education and to administer French schools outside of France. There are two key differences in the structures and the missions of the MLF and the AEFE. Whereas the schools in the AEFE network are subsidized by the French government and are mostly meant to educate the children of French citizens living abroad, as will be discussed in further detail below, the MLF is largely self-financed and its schools mostly educate the children of foreign nationals. Although the MLF schools are accredited or *homologue* by the Ministry of National Education, just like the schools in the AEFE network, more than 70% of the students in MLF schools are foreign nationals and it is up to their parents to cover the cost of their education, which is becoming increasingly expensive[265]. The AEFE does, however, contribute 20% of the budget of the MLF's twelve *écoles conventionnés*, helping to pay the salaries of school principals and their adjuncts, accountants, and a few teachers, as well as scholarships, professional development, and more. In conclusion, in the twenty-first century "the MLF, thanks to its adaptability, its responsiveness, but also the high quality of the education that it provides, is a useful complement to the AEFE network, which is subjected to severe budget constraints."[266]

History of the Agency for French Education Abroad

While the MLF incorporated the role of missionary outreach to schools designed primarily to serve foreign nationals and local people in French outposts, French expatriates around the world had been creating schools similar to the Economical School and the Lycée Français, with the goal of ensuring that their children not only speak the French language, but that they retain their "Frenchness" through education even while living abroad.[267] The goal for many, as it was for the founders of the Economical School, was an eventual return to France, or repatriation.[268] Both in the French colonies, and in the post-colonial world, these schools relied upon official links to France, to the Ministry of Education and to the French curriculum for legitimacy and recognition.

In the wake of decolonization, there emerged a growing need to better organize the myriad of small French schools that had cropped up throughout the colonies and beyond, including schools like the Lycée Français de New York which saw a dramatic increase in enrollment. The Council of French Citizens Abroad (Conseil supérieur des Français de l'étranger) was replaced by the Assembly of French Citizens Abroad (Assemblée des Français de l'étranger), which worked on devising the statutes for a Federation of French Schools Abroad (Fédération des écoles françaises de l'étranger), while the French government strove to define guidelines to offer more appropriate recognition to these schools and support them more efficiently.[269]

In 1971, a decree provided a preliminary outline of conditions to be recognized as a "petite école française de l'étranger," that is to say a small French school abroad.[270] These schools were meant for French children who were registered by the Consulate and were managed by associations of parents, the majority of whom were required to be French. Moreover, an additional stipulation was that these schools were to be not-for-profit, and the president and treasurer of the board of directors were required to be French nationals. Finally, the "petites écoles" were supposed to follow the guidelines established by the French national curriculum and were subject to inspection by the French authorities.[271]

In the following years, student enrollment increased in many of these establishments and the framework of 1971 was revealed to be too restrictive. As a consequence, in 1979 a new decree replaced the term "petite école" by the denomination "écoles française de l'étranger" and broadened the underlying definition. This new framework allowed these establishments to be run by foundations or educational non-profits, and the schools were allowed to welcome non-French students. The new regulations also somewhat loosened pedagogical standards by restricting its focus to the French section within these schools: as long as the official national French curriculum was applied in this section and led to students obtaining French diplomas, the school was regarded as an "école française."[272]

The official approval system, which still stands today, was set up in 1975 and was based on a decision by the Commission on Education (Commission de l'enseignement). It led to the creation of the National Association of French Schools Abroad (Association nationale des écoles françaises à l'étranger or ANEFE) on the impetus of Jacques Habert and with the consent of the Ministry of Education and the Ministry of Foreign Affairs. The Act of July 11th 1975 (also known as the *loi Haby*, named after then-Minister of National Education René Haby) and its implementing decrees—specifically the decree of July 13th 1977 on French education abroad—fine-tuned the official curriculum that was to be taught in this network of schools.[273] The Loi Haby played an important part in the standardization of the French national education system, building on the precedent of the Jules Ferry laws of 1882, particularly at the middle-school level and above. Moreover, this piece of legislation became the reference by which the French Ministry of Education, in collaboration with the Ministry of Foreign Affairs, determined the list of accredited French schools around the world each year.[274] It also fleshed out the terminology relative to these schools to better reflect the level of education provided: establishments could be referred to as *collège* (middle school) and *lycée* (high school) when these higher grades were opened and accredited.

The decree of July 13th 1977[275] listed the conditions under which a school abroad would be accredited by the French Ministry of National Education. Some of these conditions included that the school be open to French children living with their families outside of France; that the schools conform to French laws regarding their curriculum, within the constraints imposed by the local legal framework; and that an academic record be created and maintained for every student based on the model of those used in France. Moreover, the decree indicates that a list of officially recognized schools would be established by the Minister of Education along with the Minister of Foreign Affairs, to be revised annually.[276] Although legislation was amended throughout the 1980s, the standards that defined French education abroad remained the same until the 1990s.

No significant change was made to the way the international network of French schools was coordinated until 1990, when the AEFE was created. The Act of July 6th 1990 was momentous as it enacted the clear institutionalization of French education abroad under the authority not of the Ministry of National Education but of the Ministry of Foreign Affairs. The AEFE was established as a public government institution, and whereas the ANEFE's primary partner was the Ministry of Education, this new piece of legislation put the responsibility for French education across the world on the Ministry of Foreign Affairs.[277] This rendered explicit the way French education was and still is regarded by the French government not only as an academic apparatus, but as a vehicle for cultural and political influence. Tellingly, the opening statements of the 2003 report of the *Conseil Economique et Social* re-emphasizes that the international network of French schools is defined by its two main goals, inscribed in the founding Act of July 6th 1990: provide quality education to French expatriates and disseminate the French language and French culture by welcoming non-nationals in these schools.[278] Article 2 of the act clarifies these ambitions with special emphasis to extending French education to non-nationals:

Art. 2. – The purpose of the Agency is:

To carry out the duties of the civil service relative to the education of children of French nationality living abroad.

To contribute to the cooperation between French and foreign education systems to the benefit of French students and foreigners.

To grow the influence of the French language and French culture abroad, especially by welcoming foreign students.[279]

Moreover, the founding documents of the organization make clear that an important motivation for the founding of the AEFE was the centralization of French education abroad:

Before the Agency was created, the network of French education abroad was characterized by its decentralized organization. Power was concentrated in the hands of school principals, who had much more authority than their counterparts in France. The Ministry of Foreign Affairs intervened only minimally. The only thing granting any kind of coherence to this disparate system of the label of "French education" that was granted by the Ministry of National Education [trans.].[280]

This new effort at centralization and control from Paris was to have an important impact on schools such as the Lycée Français de New York, as will be discussed below.[281]

Structure and Organization of the Agency

Today, the AEFE is a public institution operating under the authority of the French Ministry of Foreign Affairs. According to its website, the AEFE has a dual mission: firstly, to educate the children of French families living abroad and secondly, to help promote the spread of French language and culture throughout the world by educating children in 137 countries, who represent around 60% of the total enrollment in the AEFE network.[282]

The principle of *homologation*—the process by which AEFE schools are accredited by the French Ministry of National Education—is the organizing feature of the AEFE network. According to the AEFE, the accreditation process ensures that its schools can guarantee a high quality of education by sharing the same curriculum, pedagogical objectives, and organizational rules as the French public school system. Moreover, accreditation by the Ministry of National Education guarantees a high degree of standardization among schools no matter where they may be located in the world, thereby ensuring that a student can easily transfer between schools without taking a placement exam, as long as space is available. This last provision is particularly important for the children of French families living abroad, many of whom need to be able to reintegrate the public-school system when they return to France. In order to ensure that each school meets the standards for accreditation, schools in the AEFE network are subject to regular inspections by French education officials. This governmental recognition and oversight add significantly to the legitimacy of the schools, especially for French and international families who might be moving among French schools in different countries. Even the format of school report cards (*livret scolaire*) which have only recently been digitized, continues to be uniform throughout the French system. One AEFE official described a harrowing mission by an AEFE employee who was assigned to rescue the *livrets scolaires* that had been left behind at a school in Africa forced to close abruptly following local unrest, a striking testament to the importance of these documents in the eyes of French government officials (children and their families had been evacuated earlier).[283] As a public institution, the AEFE is governed by a board of directors, including representatives from the Ministry of National Education and the Ministry of Foreign Affairs, among others.

Categorization of Schools in the AEFE Network

Schools in the AEFE network can be grouped into three categories. Those in the first group are said to be "en gestion directe" (EGD), that is to say they are directly administered by the AEFE and follow the same rules and regulations as schools in French public system. Those in the second group are "conventionné," that is to say schools that are governed by local rules and regulations, but which have signed a charter with the AEFE. In these schools, the AEFE can assign teachers from the French national education system and pay their salaries, subsidize the operational costs, and grant scholarships to French students. However, the schools are usually governed by an independent board, composed largely of parents, rather than directly by the AEFE.

In the final group there are partner schools, which are independently run but partner with the AEFE to receive their accreditation from the French Ministry of National Education. As

Olivier Boasson explains, the French authorities have a very different relationship to a school with a French curriculum depending on whether the school is under direct management, contracted, or simply a partner, although all of the schools are accredited by the Ministry of National Education:

> The French authorities have a very different relationship to a school with a French curriculum depending on whether the school is under direct management, contracted, or simply a partner. There are more or less three levels of involvement: schools that are under direct management, schools that are contracted, and partners. Regardless of the level of involvement by the French authorities, all of these schools are accredited. It's true that at one time we referred to partner schools as *homologué*, but it was misleading since *conventionné* schools are also *homologué*, as are the schools under direct management. For that reason, we now distinguish between schools under direct management, schools that are *conventionné*, and partner schools. But all of them are *homologué*, at least partially.[284]

In 2004, the 269 schools in the AEFE network included 74 schools that were *en gestion directe* and 195 schools that were *conventionné*. Today, an additional forty schools around the world are recognized by the French Ministry of National Education but are not officially part of the AEFE network. These schools are *homologués*, that is to say accredited by the Ministry of National Education.[285] These schools are supplemented by the schools in the MLF network, as discussed below.

In 2004, there were approximately 21,000 teachers and administrators in the AEFE network.[286] However, both teachers and administrators are hired and paid differently depending on their status. There are three kinds of teachers employed by the AEFE network, each of which will be described in detail bellow.

The first group includes expatriate teachers, who remain part of the French civil service throughout their service abroad—with a special status called *détachement* they continue to advance in the civil service and accumulate retirement and social security benefits while "on leave" to teach abroad. The AEFE pays their salaries for a period of three years, with the possibility of a single renewal. Each expatriate costs the AEFE about €100,000 per year.[287]

The second group includes teachers who are certified by the French Ministry of National Education but who have resided in the host country for more than three months. Like their expatriate colleagues, these teachers are on assignment to the AEFE for a three-year contract, once renewable. However, due to budgetary constraints the AEFE usually asks schools to contribute a portion of the resident teachers' salaries. On average, each resident therefore costs the AEFE €40,000 per year.[288]

The last group includes local hires, who are hired and paid for by the schools. The teachers are hired according to local laws, rules, and regulations. Often these are the teachers of the local curriculum, for example English and American history in New York.

Accreditation across the Network

Like the MLF, the AEFE aims to strike a balance between a centralized, standardized curriculum and a certain degree of flexibility with regard to local contexts. According to Philip Joutard, the accreditation of schools is conducted through the Ministry of National Education:

> The Ministry of Education [...] sets the rules for all educational institutions, including the curriculum from kindergarten to the baccalaureate. It not only sets general guidelines, but even goes so far as to set the curriculum for each subject, including the number of hours to be spent on each subject and the curriculum for each of these subjects.[289]

One of the great strengths of the AEFE is that every school in the network must respect the same guidelines in order to retain its accreditation, meaning that students can move between schools in the network and even schools in France without disrupting their studies or being required to pass entrance exams. According to one survey respondent, "it used to be said that the Minister of Education would look at his watch and know what children were learning at that moment in any class in any Lycée anywhere in the world". While this is of course an exaggeration, the sentiment nevertheless helps to illustrate the ambition of the AEFE's international schools submitted to a rigorous process of standardization and accreditation through a central authority.

Olivier Boasson explains that this is one of the great strengths of the highly centralized and highly standardized system of French education:

> In terms of international education policy, one has to acknowledge that France's standardized system was a huge advantage. It's easier to apply the French model outside of France. Once you've done that, it's easy to move between schools without a level assessment.[290]

Moreover, international mobility facilitated by the rigorous structure is not only beneficial to French families living abroad. Highly mobile foreign families, such as those with a parent or parents in the diplomatic corps or who are executives of international companies, are attracted to the French system for the very same reasons, even if they do not have a personal connection to French or to France. As Boasson confirms, "that's what makes the French system so attractive to the majority of these schools' populations who aren't French nationals, but who see the benefits of the network."[291]

Students in AEFE schools prepare the same baccalaureate exam as their peers in France, often with a high success rate: of the 8,645 students abroad who were seated for the exam in 2003, 94.01% percent passed and received their baccalaureate, compared to only 81.1% in France.[292]

At the same time, the AEFE has shown a certain degree of openness to foreign languages and cultures, although this has been limited in practice. This includes bilingual sections in primary schools and the adaptation of the history and geography curriculum to that of the host country. Despite the centralization of France's school system and the standardization of the French curriculum, French culture lays a claim to a certain universalism that resonates throughout the world, as explains Boasson:

> But when you go outside of France, France's educational standard and educational project, which is in part founded on

this critical spirit, it is remarkably flexible. It's a system that can be tolerated and incorporated in completely different parts of the world, with worldviews and ways of life that are as different as Saudi Arabia and Denmark, Japan and El Salvador. It's actually pretty impressive. It seems that we've identified some key parameters that resonate with every aspect of human life and culture.[293]

As we will see, this flexibility has helped to encourage not only new educational programs within French schools abroad, but also new French outreach programs in other schools, including dual language programs in public schools, immersion programs and charter school initiatives.

The AEFE in the United States

Although debates surrounding the global presence of France's network of schools in 2003 mainly focused on former colonies and emerging markets in Asia, North and South American schools occupy a prevalent position in French education abroad, particularly in the United States. Throughout North and South America, there are a total of 72 school affiliated with the French educational system: among these, 31 are located in the United States.[294] The development of French foreign language instruction specifically in the United States is viewed with keen interest not only by the French Embassy in Washington, but also by the Ministry of Foreign Affairs which has commissioned studies of the history of French instruction in the United States.

Prior to the creation of centralized organizations such as the AEFE, the Conseil de la Vie française based in Quebec City was created to defend and maintain the tradition of Francophone populations in Northern America. French language instruction which had not been widespread in secondary schools prior to World War I grew enormously with the corresponding decline of German following 1917. German had been not only the most popular studied modern foreign language in the United States prior to World War I, but it was also the primary language of instruction for thousands of German immigrant students in German bilingual schools particularly in the Midwest. However, while German was the language of instruction in these schools, unlike the French schools, the curriculum was for the most part American, and there was little intent at repatriation.

With American entry into the War in Europe, the presence of German schools rapidly declined in the United States; the federal government outlawed the importation of German books in 1917, and many local and state governments outlawed the use of German entirely. French rapidly became the most commonly taught modern foreign language in United States schools in the years between the wars. In the wake of World War II, a general push to include more foreign language education in core curricula appeared in the United States and was soon followed by the impetus to include this component as early on as possible in primary schools. This movement mainly supported language classes as elective—optional—courses.

This expansion of foreign language studies in the United States, and corresponding developments in university exchanges between the United States and France, presented opportunities that were keenly sought both by the French Embassy in Washington and the French Ministry of Foreign Affairs in Paris. The various studies, including the one commissioned from the National Institute for Educational Research (Institut national de recherche pédagogique or INRP), are reminders that promoting the study of French was a matter of foreign policy, and that cultural diplomacy continued to advance foreign policy goals in addition to guaranteeing a path to repatriation and reintegration for French expatriates.

To better understand how to maintain the popularity of French in the United States, the research led by the INRP hones in on the reasons for the language's popularity, finding that French culture is the main factor:

> Students of French are interested in our language insofar as it is an initiation to our culture. It is therefore necessary to artificially create a French atmosphere. The French tables, the French circles, and especially the Maisons françaises fulfill this need. Some of these cultural centers, permanently

established within a university, allow young Americans who wish to converse with French exchange students to learn about French customs and to learn our language in an environment where only French is spoken, as is the case at the Maison française at Louisiana State University and the Maison française founded at New York University in 1957.[295]

The role that French culture plays in sustaining the practice of French and the practice of French as means for supporting the dissemination of French culture echoes back to the same rationale behind the creation of the AEFE and the need to look at French education not only as a linguistic and academic issue but also a cultural and geopolitical asset. The mention of the cultural ecosystem of Maisons françaises and French cultural institutions in the 1959 publication prefaces the importance of cooperating with organizations such as the MLF stressed in the 2003 report. Finally, the INRP report also outlines the notion that French education abroad needs to be inclusive of and appeal to non-nationals—Americans in this case— in order to attain a sustainable model and maintain the global prestige of France and of the French language.

Perspectives and Challenges for the AEFE and French Education Abroad

In 2003, France boasted 413 schools in its global network, encompassing over 130 countries with an headcount of over 230,000 students – by far the most extensive government sponsored educational network abroad, outpacing the American, German or British international school systems which largely rely on private networks and associations.[296] However, the role of the AEFE in coordinating such a vast network has also been the subject of criticism, mostly surrounding its lack of transparency, the adoption of policies implementing prohibitive tuition fees, and the absence of a long-term strategy. The 2003 report aims at addressing these points and lays out the blueprint for the AEFE by listing the main goals of French education abroad. It does so with a view to anticipate potential challenges rather than create a framework only able to react to problems when they arise. Quoting the Minister of Foreign Affairs during the November 13th, 2002 session of the Assemblée Nationale, the report re-emphasizes the twofold mission of this international network: "educating expatriate students on the one hand, local elites on the other."[297] He qualifies this initial statement with a pragmatic view on how the network should evolve based on actual demand, even if this means pulling resources out from certain regions to focus efforts on others:

> We must examine the case of schools that are in a marginalized position: our goal is not to replace national education systems, and we should content ourselves with situations where the presence of schools is a consequence of past events.[298]

Consequently, two additional points emerge in the AEFE's vision for the future of French education abroad: cooperating with local educational systems and providing financial help to families who otherwise would not have access to the network, without creating long-term dependency. The report stresses this last challenge as perhaps the most prevailing one at the time, based on a study from 1997 by Monique Cerisier-ben Guiga that focuses on the social disenfranchisement of French communities abroa. [299] These challenges would determine the goals of the AEFE for the twenty-first century: to develop and support schools in areas where the largest French communities are settled, where bilingual programs and international high schools are not present and in locations where developing the use of the French language—*la Francophonie*—is strategic for France.

In 2014, a meeting was held between the French Minister of Foreign Affairs, Laurent Fabius and the Minister of National Education, Najat Vallaud-Belkacem to discuss the question of French education abroad and how to promote it. The report on the meeting makes it clear that both ministries recognized that the international school network plays a central role in France's practice of cultural diplomacy, and that these schools therefore continue to serve France's national interests in several important ways.[300]

The Minister of Foreign Affairs and the Minister of National Education agreed that the promotion of French education abroad should be guided by the following three objectives. The first of these agreed-upon objectives was to assure the development of a network of accredited French schools under direct control of the Ministry of Education, with improvements being made to the allocation of resources according to France's diplomatic imperatives.[301] Secondly, the ministries both recognized the need to organize a response to the growing demand for French education throughout the world. Thirdly, the two ministries saw the need to adapt and adjust their strategy to the diverse populations served by the international school network. This effort towards adapting to local contexts has played an increasingly important role in the development of the school network over the past twenty years, as testified by Philippe Joutard:

> For a long time, the idea was to transpose the French model in its entirety without any effort to adapt it to the local reality. And then, at the end of the last century, maybe a bit before but especially in the twenty-first century, it became very clear that the most effective way to build influence and to develop the French educational system abroad was to adapt ourselves to local conditions.[302]

The effort to adapt has been especially visible in the curriculum for subjects such as literature and history:

> One strategy was to pay more attention to the local culture, for example by using French and the local language side by side—English, Spanish, and Arabic, to give some specific examples—but also in terms of content. For a long time, the idea was to copy the French program, including French literature and French history. Now we make an effort to adapt the curriculum to the local situation.[303]

This adaptation of the curriculum has had a significant impact, especially in regard to the evaluation of students:

> I think this a relatively recent but very interesting development that has led, for example, to the development of dual-language baccalaureates: the American baccalaureate, the Franco-Spanish baccalaureate, and all other kinds. It has also led [...] to programs such as the international option of the baccalaureate... These are all new developments, and it's very interesting to see these schools adapt.[304]

The effort to adapt also has an impact on hiring practices, and according to Joutard, "the percentage of overseas teaching assignments is much lower than it was ten, twenty, or thirty years ago. Local teachers are hired more and more frequently, and that's one of the changes that's being adopted to make these schools more flexible."[305]

Finally, faced with severe budgetary restrictions, the AEFE has been forced to adopt alternative strategies to reduce the cost of managing an ever-expanding network of schools. Moreover, the continuous expansion of the network around the world makes the AEFE's centralized governance more and more impractical, and so the organization has been forced to develop alternative solutions, including alternative forms of decentralized governance. One notable example is the creation of an alumni association, an idea that was raised by the AEFE but the execution of which is entirely in the hands of alumni representatives and the schools themselves.

CHAPTER VII

Adaptations & Revolutions at The Lycée Français de New York

Beginning in the mid-1990s there were changes in the works on both sides of the Atlantic that would impact the nature of the Lycée Français and other French schools in New York. On the French side, both the French Ministry of Foreign Affairs the French Ministry of Education had begun a series of new initiatives designed to accommodate European-wide standards especially for higher education, and to re-evaluate overall efforts at cultural diplomacy including the creation of the AEFE to centralize the schools abroad.[306] One particularly important development in this respect was the introduction of the International Option of the French baccalaureate (*Option internationale du baccalaureat* or OIB), which allows for some subjects to be taught in a foreign language at the high school level. Meanwhile, in New York there were increasing demographic and financial pressures for the French schools to become more accessible to American students and, in the case of the Lycée Français de New York, to respond to increased pressure from parents for more involvement in the governance of the schools. These changes, especially the introduction of the OIB program, also came at a particularly turbulent time in the governance of the Lycée, resulting in transformations in almost every aspect of the school, including eventually a move to new buildings in 2003 and in 2016 a rebranding effort that has redefined the school in many respects.

Coup d'état à l'école

In 1989, following the departure of Maurice Galy, Gérard Roubichou was appointed as the new President of the Lycée Français. Roubichou was a French writer, art critic, and literature scholar who had previously taught at the University of California at Berkeley and the University of Virginia and who had served, not unlike Maurice Galy, as a Deputy Cultural Counselor at the French Embassy in New York in the 1970s. During Roubichou's tenure, the Lycée entered a tumultuous period, as tensions emerged between the school's parents and its administration and the board of trustees. These tensions culminated with Roubichou's dismissal in 1998 after a protracted battle with the school's parent association (Association des parents d'élèves du LFNY or APEL) and ultimately the involvement of the French consular authorities.

In *Coup d'état à l'école: politique, ambitions et règlement de comptes dans une communauté scolaires aux États-Unis,*[307] Roubichou provides a detailed account of the events that led to his dismissal as President of the LFNY, spanning a period from 1989 to 1998. The meticulous unraveling of this autobiographical narrative mainly focuses on the internal politics of the community of parents, teachers and members of the board of trustees. This focus is largely explained by the status of the school as a private American educational institution. Like his predecessor Maurice Galy, Gérard Roubichou repeatedly insists upon this distinct status as a source of confusion and contention not only for many members of the French community in New York but especially for French nationals in France, including elected officials, echoing the antagonism between the Lycée and the consular authorities that had plagued the school during the Galy years. As a 1996 *New York Times* article puts it, the clash between Roubichou and the parent association reflected the school's ambiguous identity:

Is it an American school, or a French school? Does it represent the perpetuation of the dignity of high French culture, or does it simply offer a private education at bargain prices?[308] Tellingly, the dispute pitting Roubichou against the parent association APEL escalated to such heights that the French authorities, including then French Ambassador to the United States, François Bujon de l'Estang, became involved. In other words, the internal politics of a private American institution permeated French diplomacy—both officially and, according to Roubichou, behind closed doors.

From the onset, Roubichou clarifies the nature of the relationship between an institution like the LFNY with the French government. Echoing a theme that has appeared time and time again in this research, he emphasizes the fact that the school exists as an indispensable partner with the French government, serving the public service mission to provide education to expatriates while also serving a larger mission of cultural diplomacy, even though the ties between the State and the school might be invisible. However, he also insists on the school's independence from the French authorities:

> People are quick to forget or avoid mentioning the fact that this network is for the most part made of foreign, local institutions that are for the most part private. They help the French state carry out its public service mission, in particular that of the education of young French citizens living abroad according to the French program of study, but they are not entirely dependent on it. For those schools that did not formalize their relationship with France by signing a charter, as is the case with the Lycée Français de New York, the French authorities are not allowed to intervene in their administrative and financial management, which is the purview of the body that governs the institution.[309]

By setting the stage in this light, Roubichou makes it clear that the smallest involvement of French officials amounts to interference; any diplomatic participation is portrayed as an unwarranted show of force.

Roubichou goes on to make a distinction between the Lycée's mission and its status: the former points to its cause, which is to provide education that is delivered in French and following the model of the French educational system, whereas the latter ensures its independence vis-à-vis the French government and its authorities:

> This distinction between the school's "status" and its "mission" is essential in order to understand what distinguishes the Lycée from other schools. Unlike other similar schools that currently exist in the United States [...] the Lycée Français de New York did not agree to a "convention" with the French government, thereby guaranteeing its independent status. Until the beginning of 1998, the school's board of directors had unanimously and continuously rejected that model. Because of this, the institutional links that existed between the Lycée and the

French authorities were for the most part of a pedagogical order.[310]

Roubichou highlights the fact that interference from French authorities around the sensitive matter of the Lycée's independence increased over the twenty years prior to his dismissal, with three peaks at the end of Galy's mandate from 1981 to 1988, Roubichou's arrival in 1989 and the end of his mandate, otherwise referred to as the "coup d'état" from 1996 to 1997. He accounts for this increase in French intervention by the fact that during the 1980s the French government itself had undertaken a more rigorous organization for the network for French schools abroad, the outcome of which was the creation of the AEFE as discussed in the previous chapter.[311]

The growing tensions between Roubichou and the parent association came to a head in 1996, over what at first appeared to be a relatively minor disagreement over changes in the school's dress code. Although both board members and parents recognized that the dress code needed to be tightened, parents were upset when Roubichou made the unilateral decision to introduce the necessary changes at the beginning of the following school year, rather than gradually phasing them in over the course of the entire year as he had initially agreed to during a meeting with APEL. The dispute was the subject of a 1996 *New York Times* article that described the clash between the parents and the Lycée's chief administrator as a "revolution." [312] As that article explains, the fractures ran much deeper than the disagreement over the implementation of the new dress code, attributing the dispute between the school's president, the board, and the parent association to a clash of personalities and a disagreement over Roubichou's overall management of the school. According to representatives of the parent association, Roubichou's leadership was damaging the school and the Board of Trustees was not doing enough to correct his mismanagement:

> APEL says the leadership has hurt the school in substantive ways: the quality of the teaching has declined; maintenance is lax; cafeteria and gymnasium space is insufficient, and children's safety—in matters ranging from fire-door clearance to supervision during outings in Central Park—has not been treated as paramount. APEL members fully acknowledge the

achievements of the school, but they consider Mr. Roubichou a paranoid martinet and the board of trustees a rubber stamp for him.[313]

This article played an important part in bringing the problems being experienced at the Lycée to the attention of the French authorities. The French Senator elected to represent French citizens abroad in the Senate in Paris, Xavier de Villepin, took the publication of the newspaper article as an incentive to raise the issue of the disagreements between the school's parents and the administration to the Minister of Foreign Affairs in France. On September 12th, 1996, a written question was brought to the Senate floor in reference to the article and demanding that an inspection mission be sent by the French administration. Another Senator for nationals residing outside of France, Pierre Barnès, raised the issue again on October 3rd. The responses to both Senators' questions were published in the *Journal Officiel de la République Française* on December 5th, 1996. They mirror the distinction previously made between the school's mission and its status. At the same time, it was decided that a general inspection of the situation at the *Lycée* would be commissioned for the end of December. The inspection only served to momentarily smooth out the situation. By 1996, Roubichou was publicly disavowed by the French Ambassador, and after launching a lawsuit against the Board and the School itself, Roubichou was dismissed.

The change in leadership at the school, and especially the newly reinforced independence of the board of trustees (including a number of former members of the parent association that had launched the "revolution") was followed by an ambitious real estate project, the sale of the buildings on 72nd, 73rd, 93rd and 95th Streets and the construction of a new unified campus the school currently occupies. The new facilities, with auditorium, science laboratories and large gymnasiums also led to further changes in the curriculum, including a further adaptation of the baccalaureate examinations with the creation of a Franco-American baccalaureate, as will be discussed in further detail below.

Universalism and Adaptations

For a long time, the standard practice in French schools abroad was to transpose the French model in its entirety without making any effort to adapt it to the local reality. As Mitchell Lasser, professor of Law at Cornell University and an alumnus of the LFNY writes, this could sometimes lead to absurd situation where there was very little relation between what was taught in the schools and the actual experience of the students attending them, particularly immigrants and others who are not French:

> In the face of the diversity posed by these groups of immigrants, the French state has long adopted an explicitly integrationist and anti-multicultural policy. In keeping with the French republican philosophy of a unitary and unified French nation without distinction, the French educational apparatus has tended to teach each successive wave of immigrant children the age-old lessons. Thus, to inject a personal note, I remember perfectly well how my classmates and I at the Lycée Français de New York, who were for the most part the children of francophone émigrés or U.N. diplomats, were all taught quite seriously the canonical lessons about "*nos ancêtres les gaulois*", despite the fact that easily half the students were from the Ivory Coast, Switzerland, Vietnam, Senegal, Belgium, Lebanon, Haiti, etc., and that much of the other half was similarly likely to have had little indeed to do with Gaul.[314]

This tension between the universalizing impulse of French education—what Lasser calls "the French republican philosophy of a unitary and unified French nation without distinction"—and the diversity of the Lycée's student body is a recurring theme in the history of the school, and is something that was constantly repeated in interviews with alumni, parents, and French officials involved with the administration of the Lycée. As Philip Joutard has observed above, the French educational system has increasingly made efforts to recognize local conditions.

Keeping pace with this effort towards adapting the French educational system to local contexts, there have been several important changes to the Lycée's curriculum over the years. For example, since 1997 and especially since the introduction of the OIB, the Lycée has offered classes in English and in American history and geography using American curricular standards, rather than simply transposing the French curriculum. There have historically been disagreements over the curriculum at the Lycée, especially in history classes where some parents felt that the French perspective was historically inaccurate or revealed a national bias. For example, Don Zivkovic recounts an anecdote in which his daughter came home from school saying that the French won the battle of Monte Cassino during World War II; looking deeper into the history, Zivkovic discovered that while the battle had been led by a French general, under his command were North African troops, something which had not been mentioned in class.[315]

Philippe Joutard explains that the French curriculum tends to focus on French history, at the expense of world history or the balanced portrayal of historical events:

> To name just one example, we talk about Charlemagne without explaining that Charlemagne wasn't just the King of the French, but also the Emperor of Europe. His capital wasn't Paris, which was a tiny city, but Aachen, which isn't at all in France today. That, for example, wasn't something that was talked about.[316]

A much more sensitive and politically loaded question in France's curriculum is the treatment of World War II, particularly the issue of the Vichy government's collaboration with Nazi Germany and the deportation of French Jews:

> Every country has a tendency to erase the negative parts of its history, especially when things are controlled by the state. One well-known example which concerns Franco-American relations is that it was an American, a well-known professor at Columbia, Robert Paxton, who was the first to dare say that the French State and the French administration played a role in the deportation and extermination of Jews, because the Nazis were able to repurpose the bureaucracy, the police, the gendarmerie... That story, which is a historical fact, was not taught for a long time. So, there's sometimes a tendency in history to only see things from the French point of view.[317]

According to Joutard, the French curriculum has evolved on this point, and today all French students learn about the period of collaboration during World War II and the crimes perpetrated against the Jewish population of France by the Vichy government.

More recently, the school has begun to focus more on languages besides English and French, while adopting a more modern and Americanized pedagogy and acknowledging the fact that the vast majority of graduates pursue their higher education in Anglophone universities in the United States or Canada, rather than returning to France to enroll in a university or a preparatory school (*classe préparatoire*). Many of these changes were made when the OIB was introduced (1998) followed by more radical changes in the school's curriculum that will be discussed in the following section.

Internationalizing the French Curriculum

The changes initiated by the French Ministry of National Education opened possibilities for greater mobility for students throughout Europe, and also reflected to some degree pressures for reforms particularly in the areas of foreign language learning and science studies. In 1988, the European Rectors Conference, which included University presidents (also known as "rectors") from a core group of European countries (France, Italy, Germany, and the United Kingdom) expanded to become the Bologna Process, an agreement negotiated at the University of Bologna and representing a larger group of European nations with the purpose of encouraging greater mobility of students and faculty within Europe by creating European-wide standards for diplomas. The Bologna Process primarily concerned higher education and involved, among other initiatives, the creation of the Erasmus Program permitting semester and year-long exchanges for university students within Europe:

> The Bologna Process is an important step towards developing a more harmonized higher education system across countries in Europe. It envisages the introduction of a common degree structure, a common system for academic credit, quality assurance, the promotion of student mobility, and so on. The higher education ministers of 29 European countries signed the Bologna Declaration in 1999. The adoption of this

process triggered a set of reforms in the initial signatory countries and later expanded to another 18 signatory countries. The formation of the European Higher Education Area in 2010, as envisaged by the Bologna Process, further reinforced efforts to develop a comparable level of higher education across countries in Europe.[318]

While the Bologna Process did not impact primary and secondary education directly, by creating agreements on standards for institutions of higher education, the process for meeting requirements for university admissions needed to be adapted at the secondary level. There were already several initiatives in Europe generally and in France in particular to harmonize education standards and requirements to make the national system more accessible to other European nationals living in France. This "internationalism" was perhaps first seen in the efforts that eventually led to the creation of the International Baccalaureate (IB) organization. Although the IB was initially created with French participation (a public school in France was among the first 12 schools in 10 countries to introduce an IB diploma program in 1970), the French Ministry of National Education eventually rejected the IB diploma program, viewing it as an attempt at privatization, and perhaps also viewing the avowedly "progressive" educational methodology as conflicting with more "traditional" French practices, including memorization, teacher-centered classrooms, undifferentiated content and a strong emphasis on national as opposed to multicultural curriculum.

While the IB diploma is recognized in many countries, the French Ministry of National Education has decided not to adopt the programs. To compete with the increasing success of the IB program (which grew rapidly from 7 schools in 1971 to over 4,300 schools in 2016) the French Ministry of National Education introduced the OIB, its own international program for high school students, especially Europeans and Americans living in France, marking the first major opening in the French national curriculum to allow non-French students to take some of the French baccalaureate examinations adapted to a language other than French. Generally, the two areas open to examinations in other languages are the language exam itself, replacing the "foreign language" exam with a more advanced national exam, and the exam in history-geography, which still follows a curriculum designed in France, but can be taken in the language of the section. Some more recent sections have introduced math and science exams in another language as well.

The creation of the OIB was thus a national public response to the "private" franchising efforts of the IB program, and led to the creation of American sections, British sections, and German sections within both public and private French high schools in France. There are currently 16 such "national sections" in France, and in each case, there is a negotiated agreement with the corresponding national partner. While most of these are corresponding national education ministries, in the case of the United States and the American sections the national partner is, perhaps ironically, the College Board, a non-profit organization with nationwide recognition for its Advanced Placement examinations which form the core of the English language curriculum. British sections, on the other hand, work directly with the British Cambridge Assessment International Examinations organization.

While these OIB sections initially represented an opening for European students studying in France, they also became attractive options for schools in the network of French schools abroad, including the Lycée Rochambeau in Washington, D.C., and the LFNY, which adopted the American Option of the OIB in 1998. In New York especially, the introduction of the OIB also marked an adaptation of the French program that was designed to help retain students at the school who were not interested in attending universities in France, and who might be interested in the more American approach to literature and history as a better preparation for American higher education. Some students were told that the OIB could be a positive factor in their admission of American universities: as one survey respondent reports, "we were told that English-speaking universities would see it as a plus." It is therefore unsurprising that the OIB was most popular among American students and native English speakers, since certain parts of the OIB exam were administered in English: "Bilingual kids who are born in the United States may prefer the OIB which requires a strong mastery of English as many more subjects are tested in English".

The introduction of the OIB program was not without controversy, however, especially among faculty in the history–geography department who, in one faculty meeting with officials of the French Ministry of National Education who visited the school, protested that American teachers could not possibly teach the history geography program because "Americans do not know how to train students to analyze documents."[319] Some French faculty actively discouraged students from enrolling in the program because it was not a "real baccalaureate."[320]

Aftermath of the OIB and
New Direction of the LFNY

In many ways, the introduction of the OIB marked the beginning of a new era for the school. According to Thalia Julme, a survey respondent and an alumnus of the Lycée, "the addition of the OIB was huge." Robert Pine, a parent at the Lycée between 1981 and 1995 and a board member between 1996 and 2010, makes the following assessment, characterizing these changes to the curriculum as a much-needed "modernization" of the school:

> Prior to 1998, the school hewed fairly closely to French standards and often to outdated French standards many of which had been halted or modernized in France. Subsequent to 1998, efforts were made to tweak French standards enough to broaden appeal to American colleges and to a New York clientele. It should be noted that many of the changes were made in conjunction with Ministry authorities which used the Lycée as a testing ground for ideas that it wanted to pursue in France but could not. Initiatives such as the French sponsored equivalent of the IB were discussed with the Lycée.[321]

Moreover, Pine argues that in 1998 the school's mission shifted along with its curriculum:

> Prior to 1998, the mission, if stated, was to provide a classical French education to students in the US. Subsequent to that date, it evolved into a program of classical French education combined with the best elements of American education.

This has allowed for the rigor of the French to be combined with the teamwork aspects of American systems. Sports, community service and school spirit initiatives have helped engender a more open atmosphere while maintaining high standards. It should be noted that specific board policies were put into effect placing students at the center of the mission of the school.[322]

A similar shift also took place in the school's identity:

Since 1998 [the school] has broadened its identity to be a bit more international or American by tweaking the curriculum to include some Asian languages and adding some more American-based courses, actively interacting with American schools in sports and cultural activities, and explicitly preparing students for American and Canadian universities as well as for French and European ones.[323]

Also, since 1998, efforts have been made to make the school more teamwork-oriented with more group work and assignments seeking to develop students' strength in critical analysis. According to Pine, the addition of intramural sports and cultural activities, introduced by the new head of school Yves Thezé (2001 – 2011), has been particularly appealing to Americans, so these changes can perhaps be explained by the continuing Americanization of the school's student body. Several survey respondents indicated that the OIB sections were responsible for the transmission of American values at the school, and reported the feeling that since the introduction of the OIB the curriculum of the Lycée was becoming increasingly Americanized.

The student body of the Lycée is also more permanent than it was in the past, especially as new programs in the high school have accommodated more American families and also as fewer French companies send families on short term assignments to the New York area. Joelle Reilly, an alumnus, teacher, and parent at the Lycée, explains:

For a long time, the Lycée used to be a passport for families to go and live abroad and put their kids into a school that's similar to France. That's not what we do anymore. When we recruit, we're very clear about that: if you're coming you need to be committed. You're not just coming to spend a couple of years in New York. You need to be excited for a different kind of learning experience, which is truly bi-cultural as well as bilingual.[324]

The curriculum has evolved as well. As Reilly explains, "[the Lycée] has embraced modern practices like project-based learning"[325] which stand in sharp contrast with the more traditional curriculum and pedagogies that are still characteristic of most schools in the French system. Reilly says that she sees a shift in the French teachers' and parents' "cynicism" towards the changes being made at the Lycée and towards American educational practices: "they know that it's a place where you have excellent teachers and you have cutting-edge practices."[326]

While this Americanization of the school was welcomed by some, especially for the current school community, it also elicited some expressions of regret by certain alumni in the survey, who feared that the school risked losing its French identity. The perception of a shift towards American educational practices is shared by many recent alumni of the Lycée, including one survey respondent who said that she felt that "the school is now less French and much more international or like an American private school," again citing the increased importance of fundraising and the greater number of instructional hours in English .

Robert Pine also points out that 1998 saw a radical reconfiguration of the relationship between the head of school and the board. Prior to 1998, the head of school operated quasi-autonomously: "most decisions were made by the head of school and ratified by the board... this created an atmosphere of authoritarian rule."[327] Since then, the board has taken on a much more important role in the day-to-day administration of the school, taking over the responsibility of setting school policy while the head of school was charged with carrying out the decisions of the board. In a word, parents and trustees like Pine see the new changes accompanying the introduction of the OIB as setting a new, international direction for the school.

Prise en charge: A Radical Short-lived French Investment in Overseas Schools

Another area that has seen significant changes over the past twenty years is the degree to which the French government supports the school financially. While financial issues and fundraising had been a constraint at the Lycée for many years, a brief but radical departure in French government financing occurred between 2007 and 2010 under the government of French President Nicholas Sarkozy.

In 2007, the French government decided to take a much more active role in financially supporting its network of schools abroad when President Nicholas Sarkozy introduced a system of government scholarships for students enrolled in the AEFE network, known as the *prise en charge*. This included students at the Lycée Français de New York, who were among the primary beneficiaries of the new policy since tuition there was among the highest for schools in the AEFE network.

The idea of the *prise en charge* was to finance the studies French students or French dual-nationals in elementary, middle, and high schools abroad, starting in *terminale* and eventually expanding to all grade levels. The scholarships were to be disbursed to all French nationals, regardless of their family's income. Families had to file paperwork at the Consulate declaring any other scholarships they were receiving, and the Consulate would pay the remainder of the tuition directly to the school on a termly basis.

At its peak, the *prise en charge* included students in *terminale, 1ère*, and *2nde*. The *prise en charge* for *terminale* students was introduced in the 2007-2008 school year; the program was expanded to students in *1ère* in 2008-2009 and to students in *2nde* in 2009-2010. However, in 2010, the expansion of the program was halted as the costs spiraled out of control. Indeed, a parliamentary report presented to the French National Assembly in June 2010 indicated that the average cost per student of the *prise en charge* augmented from €3,472 in 2007-2008 to €4,190 in 2009-2010, a 20.7% increase.[328] The report determined that if the *prise en charge* were to be expanded to all students in primary and secondary school, the total cost to the French government would amount to approximately €700 million per year.[329] The report ultimately recommended that the plan to extend the *prise en charge* to all grade levels was financially irresponsible, thereby halting the expansion of the program in 2010. Olivier Boasson expressed a similar sentiment, explaining that the proposal would have been so expensive that it didn't receive a lot of support: "According to some estimates it would have cost hundreds of millions of euros. It's a significant amount of money and of course people reacted very strongly."[330]

Another argument that was raised against the *prise en charge* was that it would encourage certain schools to raise their tuition, since they knew that it would be paid by the French government. According to Boasson, this is exactly what happened in schools in certain parts of the world, especially in the United States where the cost of a good education is much higher than in the rest of the world.[331]

The *prise en charge* also introduced a wedge in between the various communities served by the French schools abroad, since only French citizens were eligible to receive the scholarship from the French government. This was also acknowledged in the 2010 parliamentary report, which was fairly critical of the *prise en charge* mechanism, citing the possible violation of non-discrimination ordinances, particularly within the context of the European Union.[332] Even more significantly, the report suggests that the discrimination in status that the *prise en charge* introduced between French and non-French students risked compromising the mission of the AEFE and its network of school abroad. For instance, the report cites the AEFE's responsibility to "promote the foreign influence of France and French culture, in particular by welcoming foreign students" while at the same time helping French and foreign families afford the cost of primary and secondary education.[333] The authors point out that the *prise en charge* could negatively impact the AEFE's ability to carry out its mission by reducing the number of foreign students enrolled in its schools:

> There is cause for concern that because of the implementation of the PEC [*prise en charge*], these two missions—helping expatriate families on one hand, welcoming foreign students on the other—are less and less

compatible. Indeed, due to the success of the PEC among French and binational families, we have observed a decrease in the number of foreign students in schools in the AEFE network [trans.].[334]

The report identifies three major issues with the decrease in foreign students that could threaten the integrity of the AEFE network, which it attributes to the implementation of the *prise en charge* in 2007. The first problem is of a financial order, since the AEFE budget depends in large part on the tuition paid by foreign as well as French students; by decreasing the number of foreign students and essentially eliminating any revenue from French students, the *prise en charge* jeopardized the AEFE economic viability. Secondly, the report observes that the *prise en charge* adversely affects the AEFE's mission to "promote the foreign influence of France" by reducing the number of foreign students who are exposed to French culture in the AEFE school network. Finally, the report suggests that a reduction in the number of foreign students would similarly reduce the opportunities for cultural exchange: "[The *prise en charge*] would deprive students, both French and foreign, of the richness that results from meeting of different cultures within a common space [trans.]."[335] In other words, the success of the AEFE network depends on its cultural and national diversity, something that the *prise in charge* put at risk by creating a distinction between French and foreign families.

The *prise en charge* had another unintended consequence, this time involving private companies' contribution to the education of their employees' children abroad. Prior to the *prise en charge*, when a French executive had his or her school fees paid by a large French firm abroad, it was seen as an attractive perk in these executives' benefits packages. However, once the *prise en charge* was put in place and the cost of educating the children of French executives abroad was assumed by the French government, companies began paying their executives the equivalent of these school fees as a bonus.[336] According to Boasson, "[the *prise en charge*] distorted the competition to hire the best executives between French and foreign companies." [337] Similarly, Joelle Reilly believes that "[Sarkozy] created this kick-back for companies" and that the purpose of the *prise en charge* was ultimately to "help companies with their expat personnel." [338] The 2010 parliamentary report agrees with these assessments, with the authors noting that "private companies are likely to benefit from the fact that [the *prise en charge*] will do away with their responsibility to—indirectly—finance the network [trans.]." [339] The report also notes the inequity of a system under which high-income and low-income families are treated alike, as well as the exclusion of families with children in the primary system regardless of their income, since primary school was not covered by the *prise en charge*.

The reactions to the *prise en charge* at the LFNY were mixed. On one hand, many members of the Lycée community articulated similar criticisms of the *prise en charge* as those leveled by the 2010 parliamentary report. For instance, Stephan Haimo, the Chairman of the Board of Trustees, explains that "it did something horrible in the sense that it made a distinction between those who were French and those who were not, those who were paying tuition and those who weren't." [340] He was also critical of the way the *prise en charge* acted as an unintended subsidy for French companies abroad: "[the *prise en charge*] was a disguised bit of corporate welfare in some respects, because some of the benefactors were French corporations who should have been paying... they got a free ride." [341]

On the other hand, the *prise en charge* was truly a boon for middle-class families with children enrolled in the Lycée, especially those with more than one child. Joelle Reilly, a former student, teacher, and parent at the Lycée, falls into this group. As she explains, "if you were a middle-class family, this was huge, because it really alleviated the pressure of paying that tuition for three years." [342] Again, this was particularly true in the United States, where the typical cost of attending a French school was significantly higher than in many other parts of the world: in 2016-2017, the tuition of the Lycée Français de New York was over $36,000 per year plus fees. The *prise en charge* was eventually repealed by an act of Parliament in July 2012, shortly after President François Hollande took office, and replaced by a system of scholarships.

The Lycée Français in the 21st Century

As of 2017, the LFNY boasts an enrollment of more than 1,300, with students from nearly 50 different nationalities enrolled in pre-K through 12th grade. The school continues to follow the French curriculum and is accredited by the French Ministry of Education up through the baccalaureate, but also offers the international option of the French baccalaureate, the French-American baccalaureate, and an American high school diploma.

Although the LFNY retains its close relationship with French language and French culture, in recent years the school has adopted an increasingly global outlook. This is reflected in its new mission statement, which explains that the school aims to create "citizens of culture and courage" who are "at home in the world," all while maintaining its commitment to bilingual French and American education of the highest standard.[343]

As head of school, Sean Lynch explains that this focus on culture is a specifically French idea, but one which the school wished to expand beyond the traditional confines of the hexagon. Lynch describes his vision for the school as a series of concentric circles emanating from the core of French language and French culture that the Lycée has always embraced—a vision that is very similar to the idea of *"rayonnement"* that permeates France's cultural diplomacy:

> It's culture with a big C. It's an idea that is definitely inherited from France, that knowledge matters. [...] This is so important for us, that our students know what Culture is, the value that it can have in their lives and the world, the importance of carrying it forward. It's also culture(s). It's not just French culture. What we've been trying to do over the last several years is broaden it to include Francophonie. That really matters for us. That's the first concentric circle around French culture, so to speak.[344]

In expanding the idea of French culture to include Francophonie, the Lycée is continuing its long tradition of serving French-speaking populations coming from outside of France, especially African diplomats and other Francophones in New York City, including the city's significant Haitian population.

Lynch goes on to explain that "the next circle is our local context in New York," a primarily English-speaking but also cosmopolitan city:

> It's predominantly American but it's also the various other people with different origins who come to us and bring something to the experience. If you look at the OIB, [...] it's definitely broadening the reach without ever abandoning the commitment [to French education].[345]

Indeed, the changes to the baccalaureate and the various adaptations described in this chapter have made it possible for the Lycée to offer more hours of instruction in English and to adopt an increasingly American style of pedagogy, all while following the guidelines of the French national curriculum.

While acknowledging these significant changes to the culture and curriculum of the school—especially the school's increasingly global outlook and its integration of American educational practices—Lynch insists that the LFNY will never abandon its commitment to the promotion of French language and French culture. For example, the school decided against adopting an IB program, despite the popularity of the program at top schools around the world:

> I'm not in favor of the IB at all for our school. I believe that it would somehow run the risk of undermining what is so important for us, which is our French identity. It's not out of blind patriotism that I say that, it's out of the deep belief that French education has something unique to offer and we don't want to dilute it in the IB, as great as the IB is.[346]

In other words, the LFNY remains a French school at its core, while cultivating an increasingly global and international outlook. Similarly, the school has adopted more American educational practices without ever losing sight of its commitment to French language and French culture.

In addition, the LFNY has seen major changes to both its curriculum and its institutional culture, which according to Lynch "was predicated on the belief that our education needed to be student-centered."[347] For example, Lynch explains that the LFNY has seen a "radical change to go much more towards project-based learning, which is interdisciplinary and has a lot of student agency in it that is rooted in real-world issues."[348] To support the project-based learning initiative the LFNY has built maker spaces and media labs in its new building. At the same time, Lynch insists that these educational innovations never go against the school's core commitment to French education: "We don't want to lose the so-called rigor of the French curriculum but we want it to be far more progressive than anything you would imagine."[349] However, like his predecessors Maurice Galy and Gérard Roubichou, Sean Lynch insists on the complete autonomy of the school vis-à-vis the French authorities, despite sharing similar values and a similar commitment to French education:

> Our connections with the French authorities are more implicit. We know we speak the same language and share the same values, but we don't work on very many projects together. We're very autonomous. We are an independent school; we do not take cues from anybody. We don't. We make our own decisions. All the reforms that I've mentioned to you, we did those on our own.[350]

This degree of autonomy gives the LFNY a great deal of flexibility in implementing its own curriculum and pedagogical methods, while following guidelines set by the French Ministry of National Education. Some even suggest that the school is able to serve as a testing ground for the Ministry, implementing cutting-edge educational practices that would never be accepted in France, or at least not yet.[351]

The shift towards project-based learning was accompanied by a renegotiation of teacher contracts, including large raises for many faculty members and a shift to an all-day schedule, something unheard of in France where teachers are only expected to be present during their own classes and do not assume any additional roles in advising or tutoring students. According to Robert Pine, some of these changes had already been taking shape under Yves Thezé, a former head of school:

> When Yves was recruiting, he told teachers what was expected: your presence in the school will be x and you will be

expected to be a mentor to your students and you will be expected to have one-on-one time with them. This is your role as a teacher. Your role is not just to sit up there and have a *surveillant* do the discipline. Your role is to be available.[352]

The change to an 8 to 4 schedule for teachers was particularly contentious, but Lynch insists that "we absolutely needed a schedule that was based on student needs and possibilities rather than faculty needs and requests."[353] Some of these changes have also taken place in schools in France, especially during the tenure of Jean-Michel Blanquer, the Education Minister appointed by Emmanuel Macron in 2017 whose reforms have perhaps confirmed Robert Pine's opinion that sometimes schools abroad can serve as a testing ground for changes in France.

CHAPTER VIII

New Publics, New Directions in French Schools: Heritage Language Programs & Dual Language Programs

I began my 30th year at the Lycée Français de New York in the fall of 2002 and began to consider the possibility of exploring new endeavors. In many ways, the timing would be right. The Lycée itself was completing construction of new buildings and would be moving the following year. Both of my children had made transitions to another high school after spending more than 12 years at the Lycée, becoming completely fluent in French in the process, but ready to discover what an American approach might offer them. Even my husband, who had served a five-year term as a trustee, had recently stepped down. So, as the school began a new chapter in new buildings and eventually with a new head of school, I retired in June 2003 and began to consider what new options might be of interest.

The timing was right in many respects, as I was to discover. In France, there was an increasing interest by the Ministry of Foreign Affairs in developing initiatives within the communities of Francophone immigrants in the United States, immigrants who, especially for financial reasons, would not have access to the private schools like the Lycée. A conversation with then French Cultural Counselor Jean-René Gehan over dinner led to meetings with the French education attaché in New York, Fabrice Jaumont, and Chantal Manes, who headed the education office of the French Embassy in Washington. Meetings followed with professors from NYU interested in launching bilingual programs, and finally meetings with the principal and with Francophone students from West Africa at the Manhattan International High School, a public high school for recent immigrants

My next career move was determined when, in June of 2005, Ambassador Philippe Etienne was able to visit the school and, in view of the general enthusiasm of the students, the principal and our small team of supporters, he created a fully funded position for a French professor to coordinate an outreach program which became the French Heritage Language Program. I assumed the role of President of the Advisory board and began work to ensure the successful funding and expansion of the program. This initiative, part of a larger outreach to what was labeled as *nouveaux publics* continues to be an integral part of the efforts of French cultural diplomacy to adapt and change.

French cultural diplomacy had responded to crisis in the past, and continues to do so in the changing world of the 21st century. From the cultivation of foreign courts and the institutionalization of French as the international language of high culture and diplomacy during the Ancien Regime, French became the language of the universal values of citizenship and the French Republic following the Revolution. From the humiliating defeat and the loss of Alsace-Lorraine in the Franco-Prussian War of 1860 to the expansion of the French Empire and the *mission civilisatrice* in Africa and Asia, France expanded the presence of French overseas and continued to promote French through "soft diplomacy" long after the period of decolonization. Similarly, the years following World War II saw a renewed effort to re-establish the role of France (and the French language) as a major power in the midst of the Cold War. More recently, the French reaction to the Iraq War and its efforts to lead a European "multilateralism" (in the words of current President Emmanuel Macron) have all meant renewals, changes and developments in the role of French schools and French language education abroad generally and in New York in particular.

In New York, at the dawn of the twenty-first century, the Lycée Français and other French private schools with connections (direct or indirect) to the French government continued to attract students and to expand, even despite sometimes ambiguous Franco-American relations. There was also a growing awareness both by the Cultural Services of the French Embassy and other French government agencies, as well among French expatriates, that more needed to be done in order to maintain the presence of French language and French culture in the United States. This chapter will discuss some of these emerging challenges as well as the solutions developed by the French authorities to continue to protect the status of French and expand access to French language programs for expatriates and others in the United States in the twenty-first century.

Challenges Facing French
Education in the United States

At the beginning of the twenty-first century, the network of French schools and more generally speaking France's strategy of cultural diplomacy in the United States faced several important challenges, including a cooling in diplomatic relations between France and the United States over the Iraq War, the high tuition and limited space in existing French schools, and the shifting demographics of French speakers in the United States.

Following an initial outflow of solidarity and support after the events of September 11, 2001, France was suddenly struggling with a diminished reputation in the United States following its refusal to back the Iraq War: French fries were renamed "Freedom fries" and French wine was being proudly emptied in the streets amid anti-French sentiment. French President Jacques Chirac, accompanied by his foreign minister Dominique de Villepin (himself an alumnus of the LFNY), used the occasion of the inauguration of the new buildings of the Lycée Français in September 2003 to attempt to defuse the anti-French sentiment that resulted from France's dramatic refusal to approve a UN resolution in favor of military intervention in Iraq in the spring of 2003. In his speech, Chirac commented: "Events over the past few months have led to tension in relations between our countries. I want to share my personal conviction with all of you, however, that the friendship between France and the United States is deeply rooted in our history," he told several hundred parents, teachers, and French and American dignitaries, and that "this friendship between our people will always prevail over our differences."[354] He also called the Lycée Français of New York a symbol of the deep bonds uniting the two countries.

Despite the momentary anti-French sentiment in New York, enrollment at the French schools continued to grow, and the existing private schools with full French curricula in New York were faced with space limitations. Despite high tuition costs, the Lycée Français for instance had long waiting lists for every grade from pre-K to 12th grade throughout the 2000s, even after opening a new wing and continuing to acquire real estate to allow further expansion.

At the same time, areas of New York City, such as Brooklyn's Carroll Gardens, West Harlem and the South Bronx, witnessed a significant and steady increase in their French-speaking populations including not only French nationals, but also Haitians and West Africans who hoped to maintain their children's French language skills while also helping them to adapt to their new English-speaking environment.

Finally, an additional threat to the primacy and prestige of French as a foreign language studied widely in high schools and colleges in the United States was the growing presence of Chinese language programs, especially the Chinese government-sponsored Confucius Institutes which launched over 100 programs in the United States in 2004, and have grown to include many K-12 classrooms in addition to university programs. These programs were drawing American students away from learning French as a foreign language at the high school and university levels.

New Publics and the French Heritage Language Program

In early 2004, the Education Attachés for the French Embassy in Washington and its Cultural Services in New York began exploring ways to attract "new publics" for the development of French language programs. According to Fabrice Jaumont, the Education Attaché at the Cultural Services of the French Embassy in New York, these "new publics" could be served by the creation of entirely new programs. For example, "French for Spanish speakers" was one idea promoted by the Embassy in Washington and geared towards California public schools, which were seeing a decline in French in comparison to Mandarin. Another target audience was the growing population of Francophone students already in the United States and especially in New York, Miami, and Boston, who were not being adequately served by the existing French as a second language programs designed primarily for American students in American public schools.

In November 2004, representatives from the French Embassy, various foundations, and New York University met in order to plan a project to serve these recent francophone immigrants within public high schools in New York. The French Heritage Language Program (FHLP), launched in 2005 as a partnership between the French Embassy and the French American Cultural Exchange (FACE) Foundation, was the result of this plan aimed at offering linguistic and cultural enrichment while also facilitating English language acquisition by students of Francophone origin studying in New York public schools. This private-public partnership still exists today: While the FHLP receives direct support from the French government, which pays the salary of a national coordinator at the French Embassy in New York, it also depends on various public-private partnerships with schools and other organizations, including private foundations. As is also the case for the Lycée and other French private schools, students are invited regularly to the French Embassy for graduation ceremonies and awards, as well as other events.

The program's main objective was to promote bilingualism by helping students maintain or develop linguistic proficiency in French and keep a connection to their respective cultures and identities, while increasing their opportunities for success in their new environment. The creation of the FHLP thus expanded the outreach for French language programs to a new group of students who could not possibly afford the high tuitions of the French private schools in New York, but who also expressed enthusiasm for maintaining their French language skills. Most of these students, whether from Haiti, Mali, Senegal, Ivory Coast or other West African countries, had experienced most of their early education in French, and so were also largely not being served by French as a second language classes typically found in American high schools.

Manhattan International High School, a school which specifically serves only new immigrants who are English Language Learners, was the first to launch the FHLP, initially as an after-school option in the fall of 2005. Some of the students of Manhattan International High School were refugees from African countries such as the

Democratic Republic of Congo, Guinea, Sierra Leone, Mali and the Ivory Coast, whose education has been interrupted by war. These students were struggling to acquire basic literacy skills in English, and the high school principals welcomed the opportunity the French program provided to facilitate the acquisition of literacy and ultimately improve their skills in English.

In the spring of 2005, a series of encounters with students and staff from the high school shed light on the importance of such a program for students. Many students felt like they were "losing" their French or having trouble acquiring higher linguistic skills that would allow them to succeed in a French-speaking environment; many students expressed their desire to return to their home country in the future; all hoped to pursue their studies after high school. [355] French proficiency could be a major asset for students who wish to continue their studies in Quebec, France, or in their French-speaking homelands, such as Senegal, Mali, or Haiti.

Another initiative to reach out to Francophone neighborhoods began in 2008 under the direction of a group of French expatriate families joined by Katrine Watkins, formerly the head of the French American School of New York (FASNY) and a former teacher at the Lycée Français de New York. Watkins proposed the creation of a New York French-American Charter School (NYFACS) to be located in a neighborhood with a significant Francophone population, which could offer French immersion as well as heritage language support. With the help and support of the French Embassy and a group of dedicated parents who had formed an organization called French Education in New York (Éducation en français à New York or EFNY), they began organizing roundtable discussions about forming a free public bilingual French program in the summer of 2008. Many had already been actively involved in creating after school programs for their own children, with help from various French government agencies, including a special grant for "French Mother-Tongue Programs."

As the first French bilingual charter school in the United States, NYFACS received official approval from the New York Board of Regents in September 2009 and opened its first classes in September

2010. Located in Harlem in a neighborhood with many West African immigrant families (often called "Little Senegal") the charter school has grown to include all elementary grades (pre-K to 5) and has had its charter renewed by the State of New York.

NYFACS follows a double immersion program, offering a bilingual and multicultural curriculum. The school served 150 students in grades K to 2 during its first year of instruction and grew to 300 students in grades K to 5 in year five, and eventually hopes to serve students through grade twelve. By 2018 it had begun to search for new space for this expansion. NYFACS serves a diverse group of students with various home languages in a manner reflective of Community School District 5: 20% French; 40% English; 10% Spanish; and 30% from bilingual homes, including French, English, Haitian Creole, Wolof, Bambara, and other West African languages.

The stated mission of NYFACS is "to develop bilingual, biliterate global citizens who will be the leaders of tomorrow."[356] The school seeks to blend the rigorous standards of learning that are characteristic of the French educational system with American approaches that value individuality and critical thinking. From grades K to 3, instruction is 75 to 80% in French (French reading and writing, science, social studies, art, music) and 20 to 25% in English (English reading and writing, mathematics, English as a second language, French as a second language, as needed). The goal was to reach 50% in French (French literature and composition, science, history and geography, art, music) and 50% in English (English literature and composition, mathematics, social studies, physical education, ESL/FSL, as needed) in middle school.

As the creation of NYFACS and of the FHLP has shown, the combined efforts of multiple partners helps to achieve a significant range of opportunities for French bilingualism in New York, opportunities which in fact represent educational spaces that go far beyond the simple maintenance of a home language or heritage language as some bilingual programs propose, or the acquisition of fluency in a second language proposed by many immersion programs. The dynamic multi-ethnic communities that come together in creating these programs have also reinforced English language learning, producing impressive results when considering the high scores reached by these schools' third grade students in the standardized state tests.[357]

The success of the FHLP and of NYFACS produced several opportunities for French education in New York beyond the private schools directly linked to the French government. The parent-led initiative that led to the creation of NYFACS was also at the heart of the so-called "bilingual revolution" taking place in New York, according to several newspaper articles as well as Fabrice Jaumont's book, *The Bilingual Revolution.*[358]

The Bilingual Revolution

Historically, French-speaking expatriate families in New York could choose from among the City's four private bilingual schools: the Lycée Français of New York; the United Nations International School, which offers a bilingual French section along with other language sections; the French-American School of New York; and the Lyceum Kennedy. Through these schools, families sought to offer their children the possibility of achieving fluency in French and eventually completing the French baccalaureate diploma at the end of high school while also achieving high-level academic proficiency in English. However, by the late 1990s the New York area experienced an influx of young French families who could neither afford to live in Manhattan nor pay these schools' expensive tuition.

At the same time, areas of New York City witnessed a significant and steady increase in their French-speaking populations including not only French nationals, but also Haitians and West Africans who hoped to maintain their children's French language skills while also helping them to adapt to their new English-speaking environment. As these families began to explore possibilities for establishing French programs in their neighborhood public schools, a growing synergy emerged between multiple partners—French, Francophone, and Francophile. The French Embassy, various American foundations, the New York City Department of Education Office of English Language Learners, as well as parent associations such as EFNY, collaborated to develop French-English bilingual programs in the City's public schools, or within community-based organizations. With the support and encouragement of the French

Embassy's educational services in New York, parent associations have been of critical importance in promoting French-English bilingual programs and generating the larger community and governmental support necessary to sustain innovative programs in both private and public schools.

The International School of Brooklyn provides an illustrative example of the significant role of parents in such processes. Responding to grassroots organizing by ten French expatriate families in the Prospect Heights neighborhood of Brooklyn, the school first offered immersion playgroups in Park Slope, Cobble Hill and Brooklyn Heights while laying the foundation for the preschool opening. In September 2005, ISB launched a private preschool program with 16 students in its inaugural class. It now serves 200 families including not only those from French-speaking homes, but also families from Spanish-speaking homes and those from English-speaking homes who are interested in learning either French or Spanish.

Soon after, EFNY was formed in 2005, through the initiative of French expatriates. Their goal was to share the French language with their children and to offer financially feasible options for educating their children in French. They began by offering after-school classes in neighborhood public schools under the supervision of volunteers. These programs benefited from funding from the French government, specifically through the AEFE. As discussed in chapter 6, the AEFE coordinates over 461 schools outside of France, including 50 in the United States. In addition, the AEFE offers special grants to support classes in French as a Mother Tongue (Français Langue Maternelle or FLAM) where no French schools are otherwise available for French citizens living abroad. Classroom space for these programs was offered at no cost by public schools, which then benefit from the expanded after school offerings that often include non-EFNY parents. These factors (the organization of EFNY parents and volunteers, free classroom space, FLAM funds) allow the after-school program to keep their operational costs relatively low.

Seeking to expand beyond the after-school option and offer a full bilingual French program for their children, the EFNY parents began exploring options for opening dual language bilingual programs within some of the public elementary and middle schools. These parents were opposed to private education, both because of the high costs (tuition is at these schools is in the range of $36,000 per year) and especially because they had a strong commitment to public education and a belief that public schools should serve the needs of the community. Seeking a public option, the EFNY organizers approached public school principals in targeted neighborhoods and also sought financial assistance through the French Embassy and French Ministry of Education. In 2008 a group of parents associated with EFNY formed a separate organization called Friends of New York French-American Bilingual and Multicultural Education with the goal of establishing a K-12 bilingual French-English charter school. Under New York State regulations, the proposal required that organizers demonstrate strong community support. As a result, the group sought additional support from the other French language communities, some of whom had already been in touch with the French bilingual dual language and heritage language initiatives. At public hearings the organizers presented over 155 signatures of parents with children eligible for enrollment to satisfy its target enrollment. The proposed school also received 26 letters of support from community leaders, foundations, and community organizations.

Additionally, letters were provided from faculty at New York University, Columbia University, and the City University of New York. The New York City Department of Education sent a letter and posted the notice on its website, notifying the public and independent schools of the proposed application. A successful public hearing was held on February 12, 2009. The result was the creation of New York French-American Charter School (NYFACS) which is described above.

French Bilingual Initiatives
in New York's Public School System

In September 2007, three schools introduced the first public French dual language (DL) bilingual program in New York City history: an elementary school in Brooklyn, one in Manhattan, and a middle school in the Bronx. The programs were developed not only to serve the French families who had initiated the EFNY project, but also to meet the needs of a growing number of diverse Francophone immigrant children who are emergent bilinguals, better known as English Language Learners. In the four years after those pioneer programs were created, 14 additional schools have introduced French dual-language programs at the elementary level, and at least three more anticipate opening their doors over the next four years. These programs in French and English are geared toward Francophone, Anglophone, and French-English bilingual students, as well as students who speak little or no English. Each individual school assures its own enrollment. The network of these French dual language schools grew to include 12 elementary schools, one middle school and one high school by the year 2017. Despite the fact that these public schools are not part of the network of French schools, and have no ties to the French governmental agencies that oversee such schools (MLF and AEFE) the French government has taken a lively and supportive interest in them. During his visit for the United Nations General Assembly in the fall of 2017, newly elected French President Emmanuel Macron made a point of attending a special event at the Graduate Center of the City University of New York (CUNY) itself a public institution, to inaugurate a $2 million fund for French Dual Language Programs to be financed largely by private corporate and foundation sponsors including Chanel, Bic, and the Florence Gould Foundation. The fund is expected to continue to generate support for Dual Language programs not only in New York, but throughout the United States.

The View from Paris via Washington

The role of the network of French schools and of the promotion of French as a foreign language in public schools overseas continued to be the subject of parliamentary and other governmental studies in Paris even beyond the actual Agency for French Education Abroad (AEFE), which continued to expand its activities as it multiplied the number and size of schools it served. As before, there were concerns not only about schools like those in New York that were largely self-financed (while also receiving fairly generous subsidies for French families from the French government) but also about maintaining the prestige of French as a foreign language in schools and universities in the United States and elsewhere. Not surprisingly, there were also concerns about how to finance all of these endeavors. As noted above, one study was commissioned by the French Government's National Audit Court (Cour des comptes) in 2003 and again in 2005, including a detailed survey of more than 180 cities in 115 countries on all continents, including Australia and New Zealand. In the United States the survey covered the nine cities with consular offices: Atlanta, Boston, Chicago, Houston, Los Angeles, Miami, New York, San Francisco and Washington, all of which have French schools that are part of the AEFE network. For New York in particular, the responses (from over 970 families surveyed) elicited a great majority of complaints that the costs were too high, and government scholarships too low: "it's a system where you must be extremely rich or extremely poor," said one family which saw its government subsidy fall from 100% under the Sarkozy *prise en charge* to less than 34% the following year. Many families also cited a preference for the "more open" American system of education, calling the French education system "rigid and discouraging, with too much emphasis on rote learning."[359]

In fact, for most of the families included in the United States surveys, a preference for the American system of education and especially for American higher education among French expatriates or bi-national families is often cited as the primary reason for non-enrollment in French schools, even when high private tuition costs are not an issue. These criticisms seem to echo more general themes under consideration in reports not only on the future of French education abroad, but also in debates within the French Ministry of Education, which announced in January 2018 a complete overhaul of the French high school curriculum and baccalaureate examinations beginning in the fall of 2018, the first major changes since 1994.

According to Fabrice Jaumont, the current Education Attaché at the Cultural Services of the French Embassy in New York, these studies also led to a detailed report on the future of French education and French language teaching in the United States (2015 – 2025) prepared by Mark Sheringhman and Jean-Claude Duthion, education counselors attached to the French Embassy in

Washington, D.C. Sheringham's responsibilities included oversight of the 45 French Schools in North America, while Duthion was charged with the general promotion of French, especially in schools in North America (another department of the Embassy coordinated the promotion of French in higher education as well as higher education exchange programs).[360]

The report, entitled "French Educational Strategies in the United States, 2015 – 2025" ("Stratégies éducatives de la France aux États-Unis"), ambitiously outlines the possibilities for French schools and for French instruction for the ten years following the launch of the study. Reflecting on the situation for France and for French in the United States, the authors noted that at the start of the twenty-first century the United States was the world's most powerful country, "politically, economically and culturally" and that its relations with France have always been close but complex. Noting that even following a certain amount of "rapprochement" following the hostile attitudes of Americans towards France after the refusal to participate in the Iraq War, the general American attitude towards France remains "ambiguous." Therefore, according to these two educational experts and diplomats, the teaching of French, which they viewed as being the most popular second language in both schools and universities in the United States, should be considered as a "major tool for France's foreign policy" in the United States."[361]

The authors also noted the growing number of French speakers in the United States, both through immigration from Francophone countries as well as through the presence of the growing communities of French expatriates, noting also that many of the more recently arrived French expatriates clearly indicated their intention to remain in the United States long-term. With over 300,000 such expatriates in the United States, the report notes that supporting these families with opportunities to educate their children in French should be "the main goal of a diplomatic strategy in the United States."[362]

This determination to support French expatriates with opportunities to educate their families in French also coincides, the authors note, with the growing parallel developments in the United States in favor of the advantages of the acquisition foreign language learning. However, the report also recognized that overall in the

United States, foreign language learning is a "poor relation" in American public education, especially in elementary and middle schools, and even in high schools French is in competition with Spanish and more recently Mandarin. The report concludes with recommendations to expand the leverage provided by the largely self-financing private school networks as well as greater investment in the new public schools programs which can serve expatriate families with relatively low costs to the French government.

CHAPTER IX

Conclusion

There have been many attempts to explore and define the issues surrounding France's national identity, especially with regard to the critical issues of nationality, identity and citizenship. [363] These studies, which focus on the political and legal histories of citizenship, assimilation, and the recognition and practice of citizenship in France, join a large body of more recent work that explores additional issues related to race and religion as well as language.

My research transported these issues to the domain of education, and beyond issues of education in France to the practice of French education abroad, specifically in New York, where a longstanding and expanding community of French citizens, American Francophiles, and international elites have engaged in the practice of promoting the presence of French language and French culture in the United States through education in French schools. I have argued that these schools, dating from the early nineteenth century to the present, have served and continue to serve three missions. Firstly, France provides a French education for its citizens abroad so that they can easily return and reintegrate into the national education system in France. These schools in New York, like similar French schools throughout the world, which have been organized, administered and funded in varying degrees by the Ministry of Foreign Affairs, also perform a significant role as an arm of France's foreign policy of cultural diplomacy, promoting the French language and the "universal values" embodied by the French national curriculum to Americans or other local residents who, for a variety of reasons, choose to send their children to French schools rather than local public or private schools. Finally, in a similar fashion, this network of French schools abroad and specifically those in New York serve a global mission of French cultural diplomacy by enrolling among its students the children of global elites, diplomats, and businessmen who relocate regularly and who rely upon this network of French schools to provide educational continuity for their families.

In order to understand how these schools function abroad, it was necessary first to explore the central role of education in creating French citizens within France. In fact, the highly centralized French national education system has played a key role in the linguistic unification of France beginning at the time of the French Revolution, when initially only a small percentage of people living within the French hexagon spoke French. Schools not only helped promote the French language, but also, through classes in literature, history, and geography, delivered a national curriculum that, in the words of historian Eugen Weber, contributed to the process that turned "peasants into Frenchmen" throughout the nineteenth and twentieth centuries. While this is hardly surprising or unusual for a national education system, my research examined both how and why this national education system accomplishes its mission when transported outside of France, and even outside the realm of French colonies and former colonies, to the state and city of New York.

During the period of the French colonial empire, French schools were famously implanted throughout Africa, the Caribbean, and Indochina. One not entirely untrue myth was that the French Ministry of National Education could determine with near military precision at any given date and time exactly what lessons would be taught in French classrooms around the globe.

Examining French education during the period of French colonial expansion, and then the later period of decolonization and the creation of la Francophonie, my research found that the presence of French schools in the colonies and former colonial nations has ensured that French continues to be one of the most spoken languages in the world. As French President Emmanuel Macron predicted in the fall of 2017, French will soon become the most widely spoken language in Africa and perhaps the world with estimates that over 750 million people on all continents would be French speakers by 2050, many of them in Africa.

While the presence of French schools delivering a French national curriculum in France and in French colonies is not surprising, the presence of a large network of such schools in other countries, and specifically in New York, formed the main subject of my inquiries. I found that unlike most other bilingual schools in the United States, these schools maintain close ties to the French Ministry of National Education and deliver a curriculum designed for the socialization of French citizens. In one form or another, the schools receive financial support from the French government, either directly or indirectly through scholarships and subsidies. Through special arrangements with the Ministry of National Education, they hire certified teachers from France who are able to continue their French careers with all benefits and promotion while "detached" by the Ministry for these overseas assignments. These efforts are costly and require a considerable administrative support apparatus, even for schools like the Lycée Français de New York, which are largely self-financed.

Surveys gathered from over 200 alumni, parents, teachers and administrators, along with in-depth interviews with fifteen people with knowledge of French schools in New York, revealed many of the reasons that France has supported these schools, as well as the reasons the schools attract both local American students and international families working in international businesses or diplomatic positions in New York. Additional secondary and primary sources concerning the schools themselves, the Ministries of National Education and of Foreign Affairs and other agencies confirmed that the French government views this network of schools as an important, integral part of its foreign policy. France's policies of cultural diplomacy are often referred to by the term *rayonnement* which is difficult to translate, but incorporates the idea of radiating or shining influence, a concept that has been central to French cultural diplomacy since the time of the Ancien Regime and the Sun King Louis the XIVth.

The current network of over 490 French Schools abroad includes some that have continuously offered French curricula for almost 300 years, such as the French school of Berlin, which was founded in 1670. Many of these schools, including those in New York, Moscow, London, Berlin, and Madrid, have been sustained over time by expatriates, refugees, non-French diplomats and many local non-French families who have chosen French and the French national curriculum for their children. Some of these schools have benefited from extensive government support from Paris while others have only local support, but all have continued to offer the French national curriculum and diplomas, even in times of war when connections to France and the French government were fragile or even in some cases hostile.

This was certainly the case for the first school in this study, the Economical School, founded in 1809 by a wealthy French aristocrat, Baron Hyde de Neuville, in exile from the Napoleonic Regime in France and determined to provide the necessary French education to other French refugees in New York, especially those who had recently fled from the Revolution in Saint Domingue (Haiti). With no direct connections to Paris, the Economical School opened its own printing press and produced textbooks with classic French literary pieces. While the school, like others that followed, clearly served a primary mission of helping the expatriate community (really a community in exile) retain and develop their French identity, it also served the needs of other New Yorkers, and was in fact an early experiment in globalized education, with a board of directors and support from New York State and City officials, and a methodology (the Lancaster Method) that was part of a growing movement to spread education to a broader population by using students themselves as mentors to younger students.

The twentieth-century French schools in New York, especially the Lycée Français de New York, also provided this essential link to France for expatriates. From the founding of the school in 1935, the Lycée has served not only the needs of these families, but also a larger mission of French cultural diplomacy. Promoting a perhaps idealize image of France and French culture, the Lycée represented opportunities not only for French families to maintain their language and culture with a view to an eventual return to France, but also American families an opportunity for an elite bi-lingual education that was both rigorous and internationally recognized, but also, at least until recently, relatively affordable (much like the Economical School had been). Survey responses and interviews for this paper repeatedly emphasized among the reasons for attending the school the excellence of the French curriculum and the opportunities for becoming bilingual, as well as opportunities for some of the international diplomatic and business elite to move regularly throughout the world with educational opportunities for their families guaranteed by the standardization of the curriculum across the global network of French schools.

The mission of cultural diplomacy is perhaps more intangible that acquiring a bilingual fluency in French or a French baccalaureate diploma, but it is one that is also clearly a key feature of the French network of schools abroad. Even when schools like the Lycée Français de New York are entirely private and independently run by their own boards of trustees, the French government's interest is always present. Communications from the various agencies that provide administrative support, and even from representatives at the French Embassy, make clear that the very existence of the Lycée and other French private schools in the United States is viewed as an essential part of France's overall diplomatic strategy of ensuring that the prestige and influence of France is represented even though the strategy of cultural diplomacy is, in the words of Joseph Nye, a "long game," especially if the French education of children abroad begins in Kindergarten. The importance of this cultural diplomacy mission, which I found emphasized in policy documents as well as in interviews and surveys, reflects the French belief that French is a uniquely universal language and that French values are also universal values; there is a messianic quality to the mission that lays claim to its "universalizing" influence and importance.

While the schools serve expatriates for whom it is important that French children receive a French education, France schools abroad also promote "universalism" to often elite populations abroad who embrace the education provided in these schools. As a nation of immigrants, the United States, and New York in particular, often embraces cosmopolitanism of the type offered through the French schools that are established there.

This research, focusing primarily on the Lycée Français de New York (LFNY) also explored some of the complexities of French-American intercultural communications My interviews with a range of alumni, families, students, and administrators of French schools in New York over several generations explored the experiences of "cultural internationalism" as French, American and other nationalities live and work together in these schools. Overall and interestingly, students and families often reported experiencing this global identity more easily than the American and French teachers, who, until quite recently, rarely interacted with one another, and often delivered very distinct educational methods.

Future Directions for French Schools Abroad

While the network of French schools abroad represents a unique global institution, it is one that I found is increasingly in need of adaptation even as it continues to expand. Recent developments at the Lycée Français and other French schools in New York, as well as French schools throughout the United States, reflect this in their increased willingness to adapt to local situations. In many cases, the schools have adopted the International Baccalaureat program as a way of attracting and retaining American students who do not intend to continue their higher education in France, although the French Embassy in Washington also has launched a publicity campaign to increase recognition of the French baccalaureate generally among American colleges and universities. Working in partnership with the College Board, the French Ministry of Education also launched a "Franco-American Baccalaureate" program to allow students at the LFNY to complete more of their high school studies in English.

Perhaps the most radical adaptations occurred with a complete overhaul of the school-day schedules at the Lycée Français in the fall of 2016. Without departing from the content of the official French curriculum, the school instituted new weekly school schedules, a new semester system, and "block scheduling" in attempts to accommodate students' busy schedules and incorporate not only more extracurricular activities (team sports, music, theater, and so forth) but also more time for students and teachers to interact in individualized advisory sessions. The changes had an immediate impact on teachers' work schedules, which previously had only included classroom time and usually meant work weeks of only 15 to 18 total contact hours, as is the case in France. It has also meant that for the first time French and American teachers not only have time to meet one another and work together, but in many situations are required to do so by the school administration. While these changes were described in the course of some of my interviews and also in survey results, they are so recent that it was difficult to fully evaluate their impact, and in fact, they would provide a fruitful direction for follow-up research in the near future. This research would be particularly interesting as the French government itself has now proposed radical changes in the high school programs and schedules, as well as in French labor laws, all of which will almost certainly have a major impact on students, teachers, and union organizing in France.

In closing, I would like to cite the most recent report from the French National Audit Court (Cour des comptes) which addresses the future of French schools abroad and summarizes the continuing importance of the network of schools and of cultural diplomacy through education, while also strongly emphasizing the need for evolution and adaptation and, especially, financial prudence.

> France has a network of schools abroad that is unique in the world. Its size, its mission, and its geographical distribution make this network one of the most powerful mechanisms of cultural influence and diplomacy that France has at its disposal, and is one of the most effective ways to promote the French language and French culture throughout the world.[364]

However, the report notes the severe challenges of financing this network, and in particular takes aim at the spiraling costs of direct government support, in particular through the AEFE, while also recommending greater efforts to find alternative means of subsidizing French educational opportunities abroad (including the privately funded schools like the Lycée Français de New York).

As the report states, the network of French schools abroad is currently at a crossroads, and so researching the proposed evolution of French education, both in France and abroad will be of great interest in the next few years as changes go into effect. Nonetheless, as the report makes clear, the commitment to French schools abroad both in service of French expatriates and in service of cultural diplomacy will continue to be a priority for the French government in years to come. In order to maintain and continue to develop this valuable mechanism of influence and of the promotion of French language and culture throughout the world, the French government must be willing to make bold choices and major adaptations in order "breathe new life" into the network of French schools around the world.[365]

Bibliography

"A New Actor to Implement Cultural Diplomacy of France." Institut Francais. Website accessed 22 Feb. 2018.

"About EINY." EINY, 20 Aug. 2015, https://einy.org/about/.

"Advertisements." National Quarterly Review, June 1876.

"Artists of France to Aid Lycée Here." New York Times, 16 Feb. 1936.

Barrett, Walter. The Old Merchants of New York City. Vol. 1, Carleton, 1864.

Barthold, Allen J. "The First French School Book Published in the United States." The Modern Language Journal, vol. 41, no. 5, 1957, pp. 234–38.

Beaud, Stéphane. 80% Au Bac... et Après? Les Enfants de La Démocratisation Scolaire. Découverte, 2002.

Boasson, Olivier. Personal Interview. 24 Oct. 2017.

Bourne, William Oland. History of the Public School Society of the City of New York. W. Wood & Company, 1870.

Bowen, John R. Why the French Don't Like Headscarves. Princeton University Press, 2008.

Brodin, Pierre, and Dorothy Brodin. "A Witness Remembers: Charles de Fontnouvelle and the Beginnings of the Lycée Français de New York." Laurels: A Magazine Devoted To French-American Friendship, vol. 58, no. 1, Spring 1987, pp. 7–20.

Brubaker, Roger. Citizenship and Nationhood in France and Germany. Harvard University Press, 1992.

Bulletin officiel. 24, Fédération de l'Alliance française aux États-Unis et au Canada, Oct. 1923.

Cariot, Bernard. Quel avenir pour l'enseignement français à l'étranger? Journaux officiels, 2003.

Carroll, Raymonde. Cultural Misunderstandings: The French-American Experience. Translated by Carol Volk, University of Chicago Press, 1990.

Cerisier-ben Guiga, Monique. L'exclusion sociale dans les communautés françaises à l'étranger. Documentation française, 1997.

Charte de l'association. Mission laïque française, 2017.

Chirac, Jacques M. Discours du Président de la République lors de l'inauguration du lycée français de New York. 22 Sept. 2003.

Clark, Alfred E. "School Slapping to Bring Protest." New York Times, 7 June 1970.

Conklin, Alice. A Mission to Civilize: The Republican Idea of Empire in France and West Africa, 1895-1930. Stanford University Press, 1997.

Coombs, Philip H. The Fourth Dimension of Foreign Policy: Educational and Cultural Affairs. Harper & Row, 1964.

Cooper, Frederick. Citizenship between Empire and Nation: Remaking France and French Africa 1945-1960. Princeton University Press, 2014.

CPI Inflation Calculator. https://data.bls.gov/cgi-bin/cpicalc.pl. Accessed 10 Dec. 2017.

Crosier, David, and Teodora Parveva. The Bologna Process: It's Impact in Europe and Beyond. UNESCO: International Institute for Educational Planning, 2013.

Dallek, Robert. Franklin D. Roosevelt and American Foreign Policy, 1932-1945. Oxford University Press, 1995.

De Mejía, Anne-Marie. Power, Prestige and Bilingualism: International Perspectives on Elite Bilingualism. Multilingual Matters, 2002.

Deák, Gloria. Passage to America: Celebrated European Visitors in Search of the American Adventure. I.B.Tauris, 2013.

"Décret n°77-822 du 13 juillet 1977 relatif à l'application aux écoles françaises et établissements français d'enseignement à l'étranger de la loi 75620 du 11-07-1975 relative à l'éducation." 77-822, juillet 1977.

Deguilhem, Randi. "Turning Syrians into Frenchmen: The Cultural Politics of a French Non-Governmental Organization in Mandate Syria (1920-67) --the French Secular Mission Schools." Islam and Christian-Muslim Relations, vol. 13, no. 4, 2010, pp. 449-60.

Documents of the Assembly of the State of New York. Vol. 3, E. Croswell, Printer to the State, 1833.

Dodson, Donald. "Lycée Français de New York and United Federation of Teachers, Local No. 2, New York State United Teachers, American Federation of Teachers, AFL-CIO." Decisions of the National Labor Relations Board, vol. 191, 2-CA-19291 and 2-RC-19215, 23 Jan. 1985.

Dubosclard, Alain. L'action culturelle de la France aux États-Unis, de la Première Guerre mondiale à la fin des années 1960. Université Paris I - Panthéon Sorbonne, Nov. 2002.

Durkheim, Émile. Education and Sociology. Macmillan, 1956.

---. Rules of Sociological Method. Simon and Schuster, 1982.

Estienne, Robert. Dictionnaire francois latin contenant les motz et manières de parler francois, tournez en latin. R. Estienne, 1539.

Ferrand, André. Financements de l'enseignement français à l'étranger. Réagir et s'unir pour un nouvel élan. La Documentation française, 2004.

Ferry, Jules. Les fondements de la politique coloniale. Assemblée nationale, 28 July 1885.

Fitzpatrick, Edward Augustus. The Educational Views and Influence of De Witt Clinton. Teachers College, Columbia University, 1911.

Fortescue, William. The Third Republic in France, 1870-1940: Conflicts and Continuities. Psychology Press, 2000.

Fosdick, Lucian John. French Blood in America. Revell Company, 1906.

Galy, Maurice. "Une institution originale : Le Lycée Français de New York." Revue des Sciences morales et politiques, no. 3, 1986, pp. 379–92.

García, Ofelia, et al., editors. Bilingual and Multilingual Education. Springer, 2017.

Glenn, Charles L. Educating Immigrant Children: Schools and Language Minorities in Twelve Nations. Garland, 1996.

Gobry, Pascal-Emmanuel. "Want To Know The Language Of The Future? The Data Suggests It Could Be...French." Forbes, Mar. 2014.

Golub, Philip. Personal Interview. 23 Oct. 2017.

---. Personal Interview. 15 Oct. 2017.

Haimo, Stephen. Personal Interview. 3 Oct. 2017.

Haines, Michael. "French Migration to the United States : 1820 to 1950." Annales de Démographie Historique, vol. 2000, no. 1, 2000, pp. 77–91.

Handschin, Charles Hart. Modern-Language Teaching. World Book Company, 1940.

Heggoy, Alf Andrew. "Education in French Algeria: An Essay on Cultural Conflict." Comparative Education Review, vol. 17, no. 2, June 1973, pp. 180–97.

"Historique de l'ANEFE." ANEFE, 2017,

Hyde de Neuville, Anne-Marguerite-Henryette. The Original Drawings, Water-Colours and Sketches of Baroness Hyde de Neuville. New York Historical Society, ND273 Box H.

Hyde de Neuville, Jean-Guillaume. Mémoires et souvenirs du baron Hyde de Neuville. Vol. 2, Plon, 1890.

---. Mémoires et souvenirs du baron Hyde de Neuville. Vol. 1, Plon, 1890.

"Institut Tisné School for Girls." Evening Post, 14 Sep.1915, p. 6.

Irvine, Dallas D. "The French and Prussian Staff Systems Before 1870." The Journal of American Military History Foundation, vol. 2, no. 4, Winter 1938, pp. 192–203.

Jaumont, Fabrice. Personal Interview. 17 Dec. 2017.

---. The Bilingual Revolution: The Future of Education Is in Two Languages. Edition in English ed. edition, TBR Books, 2017.

Jones, Howard Mumford. America and French Culture, 1750-1848. University of North Carolina Press, 1927.

Journal des dames. Economical School Press, 1810. Columbia University, American periodicals series, 1800-1850.

Joutard, Philippe. Personal Interview. 2 Oct. 2017.

Judge, Anne. Linguistic Policies and the Survival of Regional Languages in France and Britain. Palgrave Macmillan, 2007.

Kagan, Olga, and Maria Carreira. "The Results of the National Heritage Language Program Survey: Implications for Teaching, Curriculum Design, and Professional Development." Foreign Language Annals, vol. 44, no. 1, 2011, pp. 40–64.

Kloss, Heinz. The American Bilingual Tradition. Newbury House, 1977.

"La MLF, acteur de l'enseignement français à l'étranger." Mission laïque française, 2017.

Lane, Philippe. French Scientific and Cultural Diplomacy. Liverpool University Press, 2013.

Lasser, Mitchel. Judicial Deliberations: A Comparative Analysis of Transparency and Legitimacy. Oxford University Press, 2009.

Laurent, Samuel. "Sarkozy reprend une coûteuse proposition pour les Français de l'étranger." Le Monde, 19 Apr. 2012.

Lebovics, Herman. Mona Lisa's Escort: André Malraux and the Reinvention of French Culture. Cornell University Press, 1999.

L'Enseignement Français à l'étranger. Cour de comptes, Oct. 2016.

"Les Établissements d'enseignement Français." AEFE, Accessed 14 Dec. 2017.

Loi Haby. Vol. 75–620, 11 July 1975.

Lorch, Maristella. Personal Interview. 4 Oct. 2017.

Lycée Français de New York. 2-CA-19291 and 2-RC-19215, 8 Feb. 1983.

Lycée Français de New York. Assouline Publishing, 2011.

"Lycée Français Will Gain From Fête Aboard Liberté." New York Times, 3 Nov. 1961.

"Lycée Here Hailed as Tie to France." New York Times, 26 Apr. 1938.

"Lycée Is Praised After First Year: Test School Giving 'Education in Two Civilizations' Is Held a Success." New York Times, 28 June 1936.

Lynch, Sean. Personal Interview. 3 Feb. 2018.

Macron, Emmanuel. Discours du Président de la République, Emmanuel Macron, à l'université Ouaga I, professeur Joseph Ki-Zerbo. 29 Nov. 2017.

---. Lancement du fonds bilingue à New York. 21 Sept. 2017.

Mancel, Jean-François, et al. Rapport d'information déposé en application de l'article 145 du Règlement par la Commission des finances, de l'économie générale et du contrôle budgétaire en conclusion des travaux de la Mission d'évaluation et de contrôle (MEC) sur l'enseignement français à l'étranger. 2693, Assemblée nationale, 30 June 2010.

Mathews, Albert. "The Teaching of French at Harvard before 1750." Publications of the Colonial Society of Massachusetts, vol. 17, Colonial Society of Massachusetts, 1915, pp. 216–32.

McWhorter, John. "Let's Stop Pretending That French Is an Important Language." The New Republic, Feb. 2014.

Minutes of the Common Council of the City of New York, 1784-1831. Vol. 6, M. B. Brown printing & binding Company, 1917.

"Mission & Vision." Lycée Français de New York. Accessed 27 Feb. 2018.

"Mission Statement." New York French American Charter School. Accessed 27 Feb. 2018.

Moss, Michele. Personal Interview. 16 Oct. 2017.

Moulakis, Athanasios. "What the U.S. Government Can't Do Abroad, Colleges Can." The Chronicle of Higher Education, July 2011. The Chronicle of Higher Education.

Mulcahy, Kevin V. Public Culture, Cultural Identity, Cultural Policy: Comparative Perspectives. Springer, 2016.

Noiriel, Gérard. Le Creuset français. Éditions du Seuil, 1998.

Nora, Pierre. Rethinking France: Les Lieux de Mémoire. Edited by David P. Jordan, Translated by Mary Seidman Trouille, vol. 1, University of Chicago Press, 1999.

Nye, Joseph S. Soft Power: The Means To Success In World Politics. Public Affairs, 2005.

Parsons, James Russell. French Schools through American Eyes: A Report to the New York State Department of Public Instruction. C. W. Bardeen, 1892.

---. Prussian Schools through American Eyes: A Report to the New York State Department of Public Instruction. C. W. Bardeen, 1892.

Peyton, Joy Kreeft, et al., editors. Heritage Languages in America: Preserving a National Resource. Center for Applied Linguistics, 2001.

Pine, Robert. Personal Interview. 30 Jan. 2018.

Private Laws of the State of New-York. John Barber, 1810.

Ray, Thomas M. "'Not One Cent for Tribute': The Public Addresses and American Popular Reaction to the XYZ Affair, 1798-1799." Journal of the Early Republic, vol. 3, no. 4, Winter 1983, pp. 389–412.

Regulations of the Economical School. Economical School Press,

1810. New York Historical Society.

Reigart, John F. The Lancasterian System of Instruction in the Schools of New York City. Teachers College, Columbia University, 1916.

Reilly, Joelle. Personal Interview. 20 Oct. 2017.

Report of Maxine Herzberg for Months of December and January, Junior High. Institut Tisné School for Girls, 1929. Private collecton.

Réunion interministérielle sur l'enseignement français à l'étranger. Ministère des Affaires étrangères and Ministère de l'Éducation nationale, 20 Nov. 2014.

Roger, Philippe. The American Enemy: The History of French Anti-Americanism. University of Chicago Press, 2005.

Ross, Jane. History of French Schools in New York. Survey, 1 Oct. 2017.

Ross, Jane, and Fabrice Jaumont. "Sustainability of French Heritage Language Education in the United States." Handbook of Research and Practice in Heritage Language Education, Springer, 2016, pp. 1–18.

Roubichou, Gérard. Coup d'état à l'école: Politique, Ambitions et Règlements de Comptes Dans Une Communcauté Scolaire Aux États-Unis.

Rousseau, Jean-Jacques. Considerations on the Government of Poland and on Its Proposed Reformation. 1772.

---. The Social Contract and Discourses. Dutton, 1920.

Rush, Benjamin. Essays, Literary, Moral and Philosophical. Thomas and William Bradford, 1806.

Saada, Emmanuelle. Les enfants de la colonie. Découverte, 2007.

Saxon, Wolfgang. "Pierre Brodin, 87, A Champion in U.S. Of French Culture." New York Times, 10 Jan. 1997.

Schiffman, Harold F. "French Language Policy: Centrism, Orwellian Dirigisme, or Economic Determinism?" Opportunities and Challenges of Bilingualism, edited by Li Wei et al., Mouton de Gruyter, 2002, pp. 89–104.

"School Holds French Test." New York Times, 9 June 1940.

Schor, Mira. Personal Interview. 10 Oct. 2017.

"Sees French Culture Continuing in America." New York Times, 10 May 1942.

Semple, Kirk. "A Big Advocate of French in New York's Schools: France." The New York Times, 30 Jan. 2014.

Société de chirurgie de Paris. Bulletins et mémoires. Masson, 1892.

Steiner, George. Errata: An Examined Life. Yale University Press, 1999.

"The World School." Avenues New York, 17 Dec. 2014.

Thévenin, André. La Mission laïque française à travers son histoire: 1902-2002. Mission laïque française, 2002.

---. Personal Interview. 17 Oct. 2017.

Verges, Flaurent. Personal Interview. 23 Oct. 2017.

Watel, Françoise. Jean-Guillaume Hyde de Neuville (1776-1857). Conspirateur et Diplomate. Ministère des Affaires étrangères, 1997.

Weber, Bruce. "Parents vs. Administrator, as Style Clash Makes Heavy Weather." The New York Times, 1 Sept. 1996.

Weber, Eugen. Peasants into Frenchmen. Stanford University Press, 1976.

Weil, Patrick. La France et ses étrangers: L'aventure d'une politique de l'immigration de 1938 à nos jours. Folio, 2005.

White, Bob W. "Talk about School: Education and the Colonial Project in French and British Africa (1860-1960)." Comparative Education, vol. 32, no. 1, Mar. 1996, pp. 9–26.

Wiborg, Susanne. "Political and Cultural Nationalism in Education: The Ideas of Rousseau and Herder Concerning National Education." Comparative Education, vol. 36, no. 2, May 2000, p.

235.

Wooldridge, Terence Russon. "The Birth of French Lexicography." A New History of French Literature, edited by Denis Hollier, Harvard University Press, 1989, pp. 177–80.

Wright, Sue. Community and Communication: The Role of Language in Nation State Building and European Integration. Multilingual Matters, 2000.

Zivkovic, Don. Personal Interview. 22 Oct. 2017.

Notes

[1] Macron, *Discours à Ouagadougou.* « Le français ce sera la première langue de l'Afrique et peut-être du monde. »

[2] Ibid. « Il y a bien longtemps que cette langue française, notre langue, n'est plus uniquement française. Elle a parcouru le monde entier et elle est ce qui nous unit. Notre langue française c'est une chance pour nous et notre langue a un avenir, ça n'est pas simplement un patrimoine à protéger et cet avenir se joue pour beaucoup en Afrique, ici.

Son avenir, son rayonnement, son attractivité n'appartient plus à la France. La francophonie c'est un corps vivant, un corps par-delà nos frontières dont le cœur bat quelque part pas loin d'ici. »

[3] Semple.

[4] McWhorter.

[5] Gobry.

[6] "The World School".

[7] Conklin.

[8] Lane 8–9.

[9] Wiborg 236.

[10] Ibid., 237.

[11] Rousseau, The Social Contract and Discourses 267.

[12] Wiborg 237.

[13] Rousseau, *Consideration on the Government of Poland.*

[14] Wiborg 240.

[15] Parsons, *French Schools*; Parsons, *Prussian Schools.*

[16] Brubaker 86.

[17] Wooldridge 178.

[18] The Edict of Nantes, signed by King Henry IV of France in 1598, was the first to grant French Protestants substantial rights in Catholic France.

[19] Judge 273. « *Les martyrs de l'orthographe.* Tous les enfants qui

peinent aujourd'hui pour apprendre l'orthographe du français peuvent maudire le lundi 8 mai 1673, jour funeste où les académiciens ont pris la décision d'adopter une orthographe unique, obligatoire pour eux-mêmes et qu'ils s'efforceraient ensuite de faire accepter par le public. Dans l'angoisse des zéros en dictée, cette orthographe, à la fois abhorrée et vénérée, continue au XXᵉ siècle à avoir ses martyrs et ses adorateurs. »

[20] Wright 37.

[21] Ibid., 38.

[22] Schiffman 94.

[23] Ibid.

[24] Joutard.

[25] Ibid.

[26] Lasser 236.

[27] Boasson.

[28] An ironic recent development is that regional languages, Breton, Catalan, Basque, Corsican, Alsatian (among others) have received increased attention and teaching hours over the past ten years, at least in part in response to European-wide initiatives such as the European Charter for Regional or Minority Languages formed by the Council of Europe in 1992 and taking effect in March 1998.

[29] Joutard.

[30] E. Weber 207.

[31] Glenn 6.

[32] Joutard.

[33] E. Weber 311.

[34] Ibid.

[35] Ibid., 313.

[36] Irvine 192.

[37] Nora xiv, xxvii.

[38] *Education and Sociology* 107.

[39] Wright 196.

[40] Heggoy 192.

[41] Fortescue 167.

[42] Ferry. « Je répète qu'il y a pour les races supérieures un droit, parce qu'il y a un devoir pour elles. Elles ont le devoir de civiliser les races inférieures. »

[43] Conklin 84.

[44] White 12–13.

[45] Thévenin 12. « Routes et écoles [...] sont les points sur lesquels doivent tendre nos efforts. »

[46] Ibid. « ... en habituant les indigènes à nos usages, à notre langue et à notre costume. »

[47] Ibid.,13. « Madagascar est devenue aujourd'hui une terre française. La langue française doit donc devenir la base de l'enseignement dans les écoles de l'île. »

[48] Boasson.

[49] Thévenin 21.

[50] Deguilhem 452.

[51] Ibid.

[52] Ibid.

[53] The 1881 Jules Ferry law established free education. The 1882 law mandated that this education be mandatory and secular (*laïc*). See above.

[54] Cariot II-14. « [La Mission laïque s'inscrivait dans] la tradition radicale humaniste qui défendait à l'époque les valeurs humanistes, qui défendait à l'époque les valeurs de la République face aux congrégations religieuses qui n'admettaient pas spontanément ces valeurs républicaines. Voilà l'esprit au départ : projeter hors de l'hexagone les valeurs de la République, avec comme objectif de prendre en compte les spécificités du pays d'accueil. » Cariot specifies that this mission statement was pronounced during a speech by the president of the MLF, M. Jean-Pierre Bayle, on June 4th, 2002.

[55] Deguilhem 450.

[56] Thévenin 25–26.

[57] Deguilhem 453.

[58] Ibid., 455. Deguilhem also notes that "a limited number of French nationals also attended these schools, such as the children of French diplomats or those of mixed marriages, in addition to other European children whose parents were based in Syria for diplomatic or business reasons" (Deguilhem 455). The MLF schools in Syria thus anticipate the diverse population of the Lycée Français in New

York. See Chapters VI and VII.

[59] Deguilhem 459.

[60] Thévenin 130. « De nouvelles formules scolaires soulignent la volonté de la Mission de mieux s'adapter aux conditions locales, aux attentes et aux besoins des populations. »

[61] Deguilhem 451.

[62] Thévenin 130.

[63] Ibid.

[64] Ibid., 131. « Je trahis ma fonction de professeur en critiquant le seul enseignement qui puisse faire de nos élèves autre chose que des espèces de sauvages. Et je trahis mon rôle de français car si nous n'unifions par l'enseignement sur tous les points du globe où nous avons une influence même spirituelle, si nous ne formons pas des Français de seconde et de première zone, le monde entier sera anglais. »

[65] Not unlike the refusal to recognize regional languages in the eighteenth century, France today does not recognize the overseas origins of its citizens. This has the result of rendering very difficult the basic task of schools to identify home languages or language weaknesses for many students for whom French is not a home language.

[66] Guéhenno.

[67] The "Confucius Institutes" a project launched by the Chinese government in 2004 now count over 260 "institutes" (including schools and programs attached to universities) in 75 countries, including currently over 44 in the United States.

[68] Moulakis.

[69] See chapter 7.

[70] "Les Établissements d'enseignement français".

[71] Boasson.

[72] "A New Actor to Implement Cultural Diplomacy of France".

[73] Guéhenno.

[74] Joutard.

[75] Guéhenno.

[76] Ibid.

[77] Verges.

[78] Lane xvi.

[79] Coombs.

[80] Nye 100.

[81] Mulcahy 36.

[82] Ibid.

[83] Ibid., 37.

[84] Senghor wrote in 1962: « La francophonie, c'est cet humanisme intégral qui se tisse autour de la terre, cette symbiose des énergies dormantes de tous les continents, de toutes les races, qui se réveillent à leur chaleur complémentaire ».

[85] Lebovics 5.

[86] Dubosclard 579.

[87] Joutard.

[88] Ibid.

[89] Lynch.

[90] Joutard.

[91] Golub.

[92] Ibid.

[93] Clark.

[94] Handschin 9.

[95] Even though the Edict of Nantes had guaranteed tolerance for Protestants in France, Protestant settlements in French colonies of North America had been prohibited.

[96] Jones 183.

[97] Mathews 216–32.

[98] Barthold 234.

[99] La Montagne.

[100] Fosdick 216.

[101] Ibid.

[102] Jones 87.

[103] Ibid., 91.

[104] The laws making English official fall under the reserved powers given to state governments which have in some cases been aggressive in implementing them.

[105] Lane 8.

[106] Barthold 234.

[107] Ray 1983.

[108] Rush.

[109] Appendix E.

[110] (*Regulations of the Economical School*).

[111] Barrett 338–39.

[112] Ibid., 339.

[113] Ibid.

[114] (*Regulations of the Economical School*).

[115] The list of trustees published in the second issue of the *Journal des Dames*, a monthly magazine printed by the Economical School press, in February 1810 differs slightly. "The trustees of the Economical School, for the present year, are: Rev. bishop Moore, Robert Morris, J. B. Lombard [sic.], Labiche de Reignefort, Charles Wilkes, Dr. MacNeven, John B. Murray, Clement Moore, Rev. Vianney, Wm Hyde Neuville" (*Journal des dames*).

[116] Although Hyde de Neuville was the founder of the Economical School, he never served as the board's President. Perhaps this was because he refused to give up his French citizenship in order to naturalize himself, although this is only a speculation.

[117] Appendix E.

[118] Barrett 339. Barrett goes on to insist that this was only a pastime, not a regular job: "This they did as a pastime. It gave rise, however, to the absurd story that General Moreau taught school in the United States for a living. It was not so, for he was very wealthy." It does however seem that Lombart was a regular teacher at the school (see below).

[119] (*Private Laws of the State of New York* 80).

[120] Barrett 338.

[121] cited in Fitzpatrick 103.

[122] Fitzpatrick 103.

[123] Ibid.

[124] Apparently, this collaboration between the French consul and a known royalist was suspicious enough to warrant a police investigation in Paris (Watel 75).

[125] Hyde de Neuville, *Mémoires 2* 376. « On peut se rappeler que l'

« Economical school », que j'avais fondée pendant mon exil aux États-Unis, était destinée aux enfants pauvres des Français de Saint-Domingue. J'avais appelé l'attention du ministre sur cette infortune.

Je demandai que gouvernement voulût bien envoyer de temps en temps une gabare pour transporter de pauvres Français qui auraient encore des ressources dans leurs familles, mais qui ne pouvaient se rendre en France, faute de pouvoir acquitter les frais de passage. »

[126] Watel 76.

[127] Ibid., 73–74. According to Watel, this was not Bishop Cheverus's first involvement in an educational initiative. The Bishop cared a great deal about the education of his parish and by 1810 had already founded a school in Boston.

[128] Barrett 351.

[129] *Journal des Dames.*

[130] This is perhaps explained by the strong anti-Napoleonic sentiment of many of the school's trustees, including Hyde de Neuville. Once again, the exception to this would have been the Chancellor of the French Consulate, John B. Lombart, who was the official representative of Napoleon's government in New York at the time.

[131] (*Private Laws of the State of New York* 88).

[132] (*Regulations of the Economical School*).

[133] Ibid.

[134] Ibid.

[135] Appendix E.

[136] Watel 60.

[137] Barrett 339. This second signature seems to suggest that John B. Lombart, the Chancellor of the French Consulate and a trustee of the Economical School society, was also a teacher at the school (see above).

[138] Société de chirurgie de Paris 24.

[139] In his memoirs, Hyde de Neuville's relation to his former student is described as "une affection toute paternelle" (Hyde de Neuville, *Mémoires 2* 480).

[140] Société de chirurgie de Paris 25.

[141] Ibid.

[142] Ibid. « Ricord n'oublia jamais l'importance du service que lui avait rendu en cette circonstance son eminent protecteur. Bien des années plus tard, arrivé à la haute situation qu'il occupait à Paris, il recevait, dans son bel hôtel de la rue de Tournon, la visite du baron Hyde de Neuville. — « Que de magnificences ! mon cher ami, s'écria celui-ci, je me perds dans votre palais. — Comment cela se fait-il, répondit Ricord, c'est vous qui l'avez bâti. »

[143] Barrett 340.

[144] Watel 76.

[145] Barrett 350–51.

[146] (*Documents of the Assembly of the State of New York* 345).

[147] Deák 10.

[148] Hyde de Neuville, *Mémoires 1* 481. "Des bals et des concerts furent organisés au profit de l'œuvre et trouvèrent un chaleureux appui de la haute société de New-York."

[149] For those who contributed eighty dollars, that number was increased to two.

[150] Watel 67. "L'imprimerie était indissociablement liée à l'école : elle employait les élèves, travaillait par eux et pour eux. La plupart des livres étaient destinés aux élèves, et le bénéfice de la vente des autres ouvrages devait servir à financer l'école."

[151] (*Journal des dames*). « Notre journal est principalement destiné à former le goût de la jeunesse. »

[152] (*Journal des dames*).

[153] Watel 66.

[154] « Onc, vieux mot qui veut dire jamais ».

[155] Barrett 338, 350–51.

[156] Deák 11.

[157] (*Minutes of the Common Council of the City of New York, 1784-1831* 292).

[158] Bourne 5.

[159] Bourne vii.

[160] See chapter 2.

[161] Bourne 7.

[162] Reigart 7.

[163] Ibid., 8.

[164] Ibid., 18.

[165] Ibid., 10.

[166] Ibid., 13.

[167] Fitzpatrick 105.

[168] Ibid., 47.

[169] Ibid., 48.

[170] Ibid., 49–50.

[171] "Advertisements" xix–xx.

[172] (*Report of Maxine Herzberg*).

[173] "Institut Tisné School for Girls".

[174] (*Bulletin officiel*).

[175] Haines 83. This statistic includes people born in France, not speakers of French.

[176] Dubosclard 94.

[177] Ibid., 94.

[178] This favorable treatment of students exiting the French system by American colleges provided a financial incentive for American students to attend the Lycée, since they would be dispensed from two years of college tuition. See below.

[179] Brodin and Brodin 8.

[180] Dubosclard 95.

[181] "Lycée Is Praised After First Year".

[182] Ibid.

[183] Dubosclard 102.

[184] According to Dubosclard, all of these men were eventually admitted to the French Legion of Honor for their dedication to the French cause in New York State (Dubosclard 100).

[185] See chapter 4

[186] Dubosclard 102.

[187] The French Institute/Alliance Française is itself part of an extended international network of establishments that since 1883 have promoted French language and culture abroad, and served foreign students in France.

[188] Or approximately $2.4 million in today's dollars (*CPI Inflation Calculator*).

[189] Or approximately $189,000 in today's dollars (*CPI Inflation Calculator*).

[190] Dubosclard 102. Or approximately $33,000 in today's dollars (*CPI Inflation Calculator*).

[191] Ibid., 96.

[192] In many states, instruction in German actually became illegal although it should also be noted that instruction in French was also banned in states like Louisiana and Maine, which had large Franco-American populations.

[193] "Lycée Is Praised After First Year".

[194] Ibid.

[195] Ibid.

[196] Dubosclard 102. « J'ai inspecté les classes, interrogé les élèves, reçu les professeurs : l'impression d'ensemble est excellente. L'enseignement est donné avec méthode et avec autorité par des maîtres dévoués ; le niveau des études est à la hauteur de nos lycées de France. »

[197] ("School Holds French Test").

[198] Ibid.

[199] The war years also meant that while the school continued to offer the French curriculum, it had little or no direct connection to the French government and the Ministry of National Education.

[200] Dallek 166–73.

[201] "Lycée Here Hailed as Tie to France".

[202] Ibid.

[203] Ibid.

[204] Steiner 30.

[205] Brodin and Brodin 17–18.

[206] Steiner 30.

[207] Haimo.

[208] Steiner 30.

[209] Ibid. The Cross of Lorraine was the symbol of Free France during World War II.

[210] Guéhenno.

[211] Brodin and Brodin 18.

[212] "Sees French Culture Continuing in America".

[213] Saxon.

[214] See chapter 4.

[215] Dubosclard 596.

[216] Ibid., 94.

[217] Appendix D.

[218] Dubosclard 597–98.

[219] "Lycée Français Will Gain From Fête Aboard Liberté".

[220] Lorch.

[221] Dubosclard 599.

[222] Vallat.

[223] Guéhenno.

[224] Vallat.

[225] Galy 380–81. « La difficulté du problème à résoudre, en dehors de la nécessité bien évidente de pouvoir rassembler les moyens financiers suffisants, était d'obtenir au préalable des autorités américaines la possibilité, pour le nouvel établissement, de donner son enseignement en français suivant un programme d'études français, c'est-à-dire étranger. »

[226] Galy 382. « Le terme d'entreprise associé à celui d'établissement d'enseignement a choqué et choque encore les oreilles de beaucoup de nos compatriotes, notamment des professionnels du monde de l'enseignement ou des représentants de services publics. J'ai fait grincer bien des dents en reconnaissant sans une gêne que je n'éprouvais d'ailleurs pas, que mes fonctions comportaient l'obligation de gérer un portefeuille de valeurs mobilières, de faire des opérations immobilières, de rechercher des dons et de réaliser des bénéfices sur l'organisation de dîners, de galas de bienfaisance, la vente de manuels et de fournitures scolaires. »

[227] Galy 382–83. « Cela explique en partie pourquoi le statut d'établissement privé d'enseignement indépendant américain qui est le sien n'a jamais été réellement admis par l'administration française même si celle-ci a toujours reconnu la très grande qualité de l'enseignement donné. Elle a toujours caressé le rêve d'exercer un contrôle direct sur son administration, sa gestion, son programme d'études [et] le recrutement de ses professeurs... Il en est résulté des difficultés qui n'ont pas facilité et ne facilitent toujours pas notre

tâche. »

228 Vallat.

229 Ibid.

230 Dodson 273.

231 Ibid.

232 (*Lycée Français de New York*).

233 Ibid.

234 This is something that has changed in recent years, as will be discussed in chapter 7.

235 See chapter 6.

236 Vallat.

237 Ibid.

238 Zivkovic.

239 Ibid.

240 Vallat.

241 Schor.

242 "Artists of France to Aid Lycée Here".

243 "Lycée Here Hailed as Tie to France".

244 Zivkovic.

245 Moss.

246 Schor.

247 Vallat.

248 Zivkovic.

249 The classes were offered in 6th grade for a number of years in compliance with the New York State Regents requirement. A minimum number of hours in American History were required in high school so that students at the Lycée could receive a New York State high school diploma, usually at the completion of "Premiere" or 11th grade.

250 Schor.

251 Ibid.

252 Lorch.

253 Zivkovic.

254 Reilly.

255 Ibid.

256 Ibid.

257 "About EINY".

258 Ibid.

259 Ibid.

260 See chapter 2.

261 (*Charte de l'association*).

262 In Morocco, the MLF operates under the name of Office scolaire et universitaire international (OSUI). In the Ivory Coast, the organization is known as the Mission laïque Côte d'Ivoire (MI-CI). In the discussion that follows, the MLF, the OSUI, and the MI-CI will be referred to collectively as the MLF.

263 "La MLF, acteur de l'enseignement français à l'étranger".

264 Cariot II-4.

265 Ibid., II-16.

266 Ibid. « Au tournant du XXIème siècle, la Mission laïque, grâce à sa capacité d'adaptation, à sa réactivité mais également à un enseignement de qualité, constitue un bon outil, complémentaire des établissements de l'Agence soumis à un contexte budgétaire extrêmement contraint. »

267 See chapters 4 and 5.

268 This sentiment is echoed in a recent speech by French President Emmanuel Macron, in which he proclaimed to French citizens living in New York: "revenez!" (Macron, *Lancement du fonds bilingue à New York*).

269 "Historique de l'ANEFE".

270 Ibid. « Le décret de 1971 définissait les conditions pour être 'réputée petite école française de l'étranger' : avoir été créée pour scolariser les enfants français immatriculés au Consulat, être gérées par une association ou société de parents d'élèves à majorité française ; être à but non lucratif ; avoir un conseil d'administration dont le président ou le trésorier sont français ; dispenser un enseignement conforme 'pour l'essentiel' aux programmes français et accepter les inspections administratives et financières des autorités françaises. »

271 The schools were allowed to deviate from the national curriculum, but were required to respect its general outlines. The terms of the decree are somewhat vague in this regard: « dispenser un

enseignement conforme 'pour l'essentiel' aux programmes français »
("Historique de l'ANEFE").

[272] "Historique de l'ANEFE". «Sur le plan pédagogique, il fallait qu'elles offrent, 'au moins dans leur section française,' un enseignement conforme aux programmes français et conduisant à l'octroi de diplômes français. »

[273] (*Loi Haby*).

[274] The decree of September 9th 1993 now determines the guidelines to accredit a school ("Historique de l'ANEFE").

[275] "Décret n°77-822".

[276] "Décret n°77-822".

[277] The ANEFE is still present in this conversation as it sits on the board of the AEFE ("Historique de l'ANEFE").

[278] Cariot I-6.

[279] Ibid., II-99. Art. 2. – l'Agence a pour objet :

1° D'assurer, en faveur des enfants de nationalité française résidant à l'étranger, les missions de service public relatives à l'éducation ;

2° De contribuer au renforcement des relations de coopération entre les systèmes éducatifs français et étrangers au bénéfice des élèves français et étrangers ;

3° De contribuer, notamment par l'accueil d'élèves étrangers, au rayonnement de la langue et de la culture française.

[280] Cariot II-12. «Avant la création de l'Agence, le réseau d'enseignement français de l'étranger était marqué par une organisation très décentralisée. Le rôle essentiel était alors dévolu aux chefs d'établissements qui avaient un pouvoir beaucoup plus large que celui de leurs homologues en France. La tutell du ministère des affaires étrangères était très discrète. Seul le label « enseignement français », conféré par le ministère de l'Éducation nationale, assurait une cohérence minimale à ce système très disparate. »

[281] See chapter 7.

[282] "Les Établissements d'enseignement Français".

[283] Verges.

[284] Boasson.

[285] Ferrand 19–20. The schools that are "conventionné" and "en gestion directe" are by definition "homologue" since they are required to follow the French national curriculum.

[286] Ferrand 21.

[287] Ibid., 22.

[288] Ibid.

[289] Joutard.

[290] Boasson.

[291] Ibid.

[292] Ferrand 23–24.

[293] Boasson.

[294] Cariot II-27.

[295] Ibid., II-31. « [...] on s'accorde à reconnaître que les élèves de français s'intéressent à notre langue dans la mesure où ils peuvent s'initier à notre civilisation. Il convient donc de recréer l'atmosphère française en des milieux artificiels. Les Tables françaises, les Cercles français et surtout les Maisons françaises répondent à ce besoin. Certaines de ces Maisons, établies de façon permanente à proximité d'une Université, permettent aux jeunes Américains qui le désirent de converser avec des boursiers français invités à faire un séjour d'un ou deux ans en Amérique, de s'initier aux coutumes françaises et d'apprendre notre langue sous un toit où l'on ne doit s'exprimer qu'en français. Telle est la Maison française de l'université d'Etat de Louisiane et la Maison française inaugurée à l'Université de New York en 1957. »

[296] Cariot I-6.

[297] Ibid., II-52. « Formation des élèves expatriés d'une part, des élites locales d'autres part. »

[298] Ibid., II-52. « Nous devons examiner le cas des établissements qui sont dans une situation marginale: nous n'avons pas vocation à nous substituer aux système éducatifs nationaux, nous ne devons pas nous maintenir là où la présence de nos établissements résulte de situations révolues. »

[299] Cerisier-ben Guiga.

[300] « Les deux ministres ont réaffirmé l'importance stratégique de

l'enseignement français à l'étranger. » (*Réunion interministérielle* 1)

[301] « Assurer un développement maîtrisé du réseau des établissements français homologués, avec une meilleure allocation des moyens en fonction des priorités diplomatiques françaises. » (*Réunion interministérielle* 1)

[302] Joutard.

[303] Ibid.

[304] Ibid.

[305] Ibid.

[306] See chapter 6.

[307] Translated as *Coup d'État in a School: Politics, Ambition, and a Settling of Scores in a Academic Community in the United States.*

[308] B. Weber.

[309] Roubichou 2. « On oublie ou on évite souvent d'insister sur le fait que ce réseau est, dans sa majeure partie, composé d'institutions locales étrangères qui sont pour la plupart privées. Elles aident l'État français à assurer une mission de service public, à savoir la scolarisation, selon les programmes français, de jeunes Français vivant à l'étranger, mais elles ne relèvent pas systématiquement et entièrement de lui. Pour nombre d'entre elles qui n'ont pas formalisé leurs rapports avec la France par la signature d'une "convention", comme c'était le cas du Lycée Français de New York, les autorités françaises ne sont pas habilitées à intervenir dans leur gestion administrative et financière qui est du ressort de la structure qui dirige l'institution. »

[310] Roubichou 11. « Cette distinction entre son "statut" et sa "mission" est essentielle pour comprendre certaines données de sa spécificité. A la différence d'autres établissements de même nature qui existent actuellement aux États-Unis (six lui sont comparables au moins par la taille), le Lycée Français de New York n'a pas passé de "convention" avec l'État français, préservant ainsi son statut indépendant. Son Conseil d'administration avait jusqu'au début de l'année 1998 unanimement et constamment refusé cette formule. Aussi les seuls liens institutionnels que le Lycée a avec les autorités françaises sont-ils surtout d'ordre pédagogique. »

[311] Roubichou 11.

[312] B. Weber.

[313] Ibid.

[314] Lasser 335.

[315] Zivkovic.

[316] Joutard.

[317] Ibid.

[318] Crosier and Parveva 19.

[319] Joutard.

[320] Ibid.

[321] Pine.

[322] Ibid.

[323] Ibid.

[324] Reilly.

[325] Ibid.

[326] Ibid.

[327] Pine.

[328] Mancel et al., sec.II.A.1.

[329] Mancel et al., sec.II.A.3.a

[330] Boasson.

[331] Ibid.

[332] Mancel et al., sec.II.A.2.

[333] « [L'AEFE a pour objet] de contribuer, notamment par l'accueil d'élèves étrangers, au rayonnement de la France et de la culture française ».

[334] Mancel et al., sec.II.A.4.a. « Or il est à craindre que, du fait de la mise en œuvre de la PEC, ces deux missions – aide aux familles d'expatriés d'une part, accueil d'élèves étrangers d'autre part – soient de moins en moins compatibles. En effet, face au succès rencontré par la PEC auprès des familles françaises et binationales, on constate une diminution tendancielle du nombre d'élèves étrangers dans les établissements du réseau AEFE. »

[335] Mancel et al., sec.II.A.4.a. « Enfin, elle priverait les élèves, Français comme étrangers, des richesses qui naissent de la rencontre de cultures différentes au sein d'un espace commun. »

[336] According some commentators, this may not have been unintentional at all. For example, an article in *Le Monde* points out

that 60% of the two to three million French citizens living abroad voted for Sarkozy in the 2007 election (Laurent).

[337] Boasson.

[338] Reilly.

[339] Mancel et al., sec.II.A.4.b. « [L]es entreprises sont susceptibles de bénéficier d'un effet d'aubaine les incitant à renoncer à leur responsabilité de financeur – indirect – du réseau. »

[340] Haimo.

[341] Ibid.

[342] Reilly.

[343] "Mission & Vision".

[344] Lynch.

[345] Ibid.

[346] Ibid.

[347] Ibid.

[348] Ibid.

[349] Ibid.

[350] Ibid.

[351] Pine.

[352] Ibid.

[353] Lynch.

[354] Chirac. « Les événements des derniers mois ont provoqué c'est vrai, quelques tensions dans les relations entre nos deux pays. A tous je voudrais vous dire ici ma conviction. L'amitié entre la France et les Etats-Unis […] est solidement enracinée dans les profondeurs de notre histoire… Cette amitié entre nos peuples sera toujours plus forte que les divergences. »

[355] Ross and Jaumont 1–18.

[356] "Mission Statement".

[357] Ross and Jaumont 1–18.

[358] Jaumont, *The Bilingual Revolution*.

[359] Cariot II-11. « Rigide et peu encourageant, favorisant trop le bourrage de crâne. »

[360] Jaumont, *Personal Interview*.

[361] Ibid. « Un outil majeur de notre politique d'influence. »

[362] Ibid. « Un objectif primordial de notre stratégie diplomatique

à l'égard des États-Unis. »

[363] Weil; Brubaker.

[364] (*L'Enseignement Français à l'étranger* 7). « La France dispose d'un réseau scolaire à l'étranger unique au monde. Par son ampleur, ses missions et sa répartition géographique, il constitue l'un des instruments d'influence, de rayonnement et d'attractivité les plus puissants et l'un des vecteurs les plus efficaces au service de la francophonie. »

[365] « Mais, en tout état de cause, préserver et développer ce précieux outil d'influence et de rayonnement de la France dans le monde, conforter cet instrument majeur au service de la francophonie, exigent que soient opérés sans tarder les choix indispensables pour lui insuffler une nouvelle dynamique. »

Index

About the Author

Jane Flatau Ross is an educator with over 40 years' experience in the field of international education, including a long career at the Lycée Français de New York. She is the founder and President of the French Heritage Language Program, an organization that provides French language instruction and support to Francophone immigrants in the United States.

Jane received her BA from Swarthmore College, majoring in history and French, her MA from Hunter College in English, and a PhD in International Education from New York University.

Jane is the co-author of a number of scholarly papers and book chapters concerning the development of French Heritage Language programs, bilingual and dual language initiatives. She was awarded the Legion of Honor and the Palmes Académiques by the French government for her service to French education.

About TBR Books

*A Program of The Center for the Advancement of
Languages, Education, and Communities (CALEC)*

TBR Books

TBR Books is a program of the Center for the Advancement of Languages, Education, and Communities. We publish researchers and practitioners who seek to engage diverse communities on topics related to education, languages, cultural history, and social initiatives. We translate our books in a variety of languages to further expand our impact. Become a member of TBR Books and receive complimentary access to all our books.

Our Books in English

Salsa Dancing in Gym Shoes: Developing Cultural Competence to Foster Latino Student Success by Tammy Oberg de la Garza and Alyson Leah Lavigne

Mamma in her Village by Maristella de Panniza Lorch

The Other Shore by Maristella de Panniza Lorch

The Clarks of Willsborough Point: A Journey through Childhood by Darcey Hale

Beyond Gibraltar by Maristella de Panniza Lorch

The Gift of Languages: Paradigm Shift in U.S. Foreign Language Education by Fabrice Jaumont and Kathleen Stein-Smith

Two Centuries of French Education in New York: The Role of Schools in Cultural Diplomacy by Jane Flatau Ross

The Clarks of Willsborough Point: The Long Trek North by Darcey Hale

The Bilingual Revolution: The Future of Education is in Two Languages by Fabrice Jaumont

Our Books in Translation

La Rivoluzione bilingue: Il futuro dell'istruzione in due lingue by Fabrice Jaumont

El regalo de las lenguas : Un cambio de paradigma en la enseñanza de las lenguas extranjeras en Estados Unidos de Fabrice Jaumont y Kathleen Stein-Smith

Rewolucja Dwujęzyczna: Przyszłość edukacji jest w dwóch językach by Fabrice Jaumont

Le don des langues : vers un changement de paradigme dans l'enseignement des langues étrangères aux États-Unis de Fabrice Jaumont et Kathleen Stein-Smith

Our books are available on our website and on all major online bookstores as paperback and e-book. Some of our books have been translated in Arabic, Chinese, English, French, German, Italian, Japanese, Polish, Russian, Spanish. For a listing of all books published by TBR Books, information on our series, or for our submission guidelines for authors, visit our website at

http://www.tbr-books.org

About CALEC

The Center for the Advancement of Languages, Education, and Communities is a nonprofit organization with a focus on multilingualism, cross-cultural understanding, and the dissemination of ideas. Our mission is to transform lives by helping linguistic communities create innovative programs, and by supporting parents and educators through research, publications, mentoring, and connections.

We have served multiple communities through our flagship programs which include:

- TBR Books, our publishing arm; which publishes research, essays, and case studies with a focus on innovative ideas for education, languages, and cultural development;

- Our online platform provides information, coaching, support to multilingual families seeking to create dual-language programs in schools;

- NewYorkinFrench.net, an online platform which provides collaborative tools to support New York's Francophone community and the diversity of people who speak French.

We also support parents and educators interested in advancing languages, education, and communities. We participate in events and conferences that promote multilingualism and cultural development. We provide consulting for school leaders and educators who implement multilingual programs in their school. For more information and ways, you can support our mission, visit

http://www.calec.org